To Ley
Best Regards
Clark Hetherington

Six Chukkers of Love

by

Wm. Clark Hetherington

authorHOUSE™

1663 LIBERTY DRIVE, SUITE 200
BLOOMINGTON, INDIANA 47403
(800) 839-8640
WWW.AUTHORHOUSE.COM

© *2005 Wm. Clark Hetherington. All Rights Reserved.*

No part of this book may be reproduced, stored in a retrieval system, or transmitted by any means without the written permission of the author.

First published by AuthorHouse 01/28/05

> *ISBN: 1-4208-2892-4 (sc)*
> *ISBN: 1-4208-2893-2 (dj)*

Library of Congress Control Number: 2005900623

Printed in the United States of America
Bloomington, Indiana

This book is printed on acid-free paper.

DEDICATION

With pride and joy, I dedicate this book, <u>Six Chukkers of Love</u> to my beautiful wife, Marian, and our two wonderful sons, Bill and Steve. Thank you for your support and love over these many years.

The memories of my mother, Helen Rowena Hetherington, and my father, William Leslie Hetherington, for their love, encouragement and guidance.

RESOURCES

Most of the information and pictures for this book came from Clark and Marian Hetherington's photo albums and polo memorabilia acquired over some 50 years.

- The USPA furnished much information and statistics that greatly contributed. _Information was also taken from USPA yearbooks.
- The National Polo Museum and Hall of Fame furnished both information and pictures.
- Mr. Ned Hochman furnished both information and photos.
- Some photos taken by Alec Pacheco.
- Marian Hetherington contributed many ideas, thoughts and the name of the book.
- Typing and computer expertise by Computer & Internet Services, Inc.
- Book written and issued by Clark Publishing, Inc.

INTRODUCTION

Six Chukkers of Love is more than Clark Hetherington's autobiography. It is a first-hand account of the history of polo in the United States post World War II. Clark knew all of the movers and shakers, great players and sundry characters that were responsible for polos growth and development. His book is filled with wonderful stories of these individuals and their enthusiasm for the sport. These pages portray not only his love of polo and his important role in its growth but also the influential roles played by each of many other individuals.

At the National Museum of Polo and Hall of Fame part of our mission is to preserve, record, and archive the history and tradition of polo. Much of what Clark has written in these pages are anecdotes of personal experiences no where else previously documented. The anecdotes and stories convey what all of us who live the sport know to be the true flavor of its tradition. Our heartfelt gratitude goes out to the author for preserving this history.

Six Chukkers of Love is another chapter in Clark Hetherington's dedicated service to the sport of polo. In 2004, the National Museum of Polo and Hall of Fame recognized his lifetime contributions with the Iglehart Award. Some of these contributions are briefly outlined on the plaque in his honor at the Museum as follows:

He spent a lifetime dedicated to polo. An avid player since age 7.

He later captained the Oklahoma University team. He started Broad Acres Polo Club in 1954 and served four years as USPA circuit governor. At his own expense, he produced educational films such as <u>Charlie Chukker</u> and an umpire training presentation. Clark has been called by many, "The father of professional umpiring". He tirelessly promoted a uniform standard for all umpires to the USPA and to clubs around the country. After his appointment as USPA chief umpire, he developed umpire training programs and conducted numerous clinics across the nation, furnishing horses and equipment. More than 250 polo players, including several Hall of Fame inductees, claim Hetherington as their mentor.

I know the many friends Clark has made over the years on the polo field will enjoy reading through these pages. Undoubtedly, they will arouse in each reader treasured memories of polo fun. For me and countless others in the sport, his career has been a wonderful influence and example.

Stephen Orthwein

Chairman

National Museum of Polo and Hall of Fame

Table of Contents

Dedication v

Resources vii

Introduction ix

Chapter One   Family History (School and Polo) .. 1

Chapter Two   World War II 17

Chapter Three Post War Polo and Business 31

Chapter Four   Polo Experiences 46

Chapter Five   Notables 65

Chapter Six   The History of Palm Beach Polo
                and Country Club 98

Chapter Seven Polo History and Future 119

Chapter Eight Epilogue 126

Chapter One
Family History (School and Polo)

<u>Mother's Words: Roll son Roll</u>

Clark, you must learn how to get away from the horse when it falls. Slipping down on a turn to left or right, very simple. A tripping somersault to front is more difficult, but don't ever stop rolling, the horse will be coming.

I probably taught several hundred people to play polo, but you can't teach how to get away from a falling horse in an early lesson plan. It would scare prospects out of trying, not to mention the wives banning the sport.

Back to polo later, but let me tell you why I wanted to write a book. Everybody wants to write a book. Why? In my case, first, my great-grandparents and family did not pass on a good history of the old family. Most life, personal history books are dull, and only interesting to the writer's family. So put up with a few boring pages. Secondly, I enjoyed the most wonderful, exciting, and interesting polo life, while loving and enjoying my family.

I was born in Norman, Oklahoma on July 25, 1921. My father came from Canada. He often said, "For a nickel, my mother could have ridden the street car across the line, and I would have been an American citizen", which he soon became.

My dad moved with his mother and grandmother to Norman, Oklahoma in the early 1900's. His grandmother started the first department store on East Main Street, named the Broken Dollar.

My mother, her father, uncle and brother came from Alton, Illinois. Mother's father had a wholesale cigar territory franchise, covering central Oklahoma. He delivered cigars to the stores in a T-model Ford on dirt roads.

Mother graduated from the University of Oklahoma. She met my father in Norman. They fell in love and were married. The whole family, at first, lived in a small white-frame house at 711 North Peters. To this day, I have never figured out, where the heck did everyone sleep? My father, mother, two great-grandmothers, mother's father, Ray Hudgens, her Uncle, Harry, my father's mother, called Pete, and my brother, Charles, and mother's brother, Warren (Warren later went to medical school in Chicago, then died of pneumonia). The family bought another house across the street. It made living much more enjoyable. Dad and mother later bought a house near the University of Oklahoma. They wanted my brother, Charles and myself to have the best education. We lived there while Charles and I went to junior high school, high school, and college. Our transportation was roller-skates, bicycles, walking and later, Charles and I bought a T-model Ford for $15.00. Fifteen cents of gasoline lasted two weeks. We took the T-model Ford on a west Oklahoma camping trip. On the way back, a wheel past us, and it was one of ours. The car went into a ditch. Two Indians came along, and we sold them the car for $7.50 and hitch-hiked home.

Even though mother had an enlarged varicose vein right leg, she began riding the government Army horses in the University ROTC Program. She became a very talented and beautiful equestrian, including jumping, schooling, and all phases of show riding. She was often called to ride top horses in shows throughout the country. She was determined and tough. While jumping a green horse one day, the horse hit the jump and the horse and the jump wings all ended up on top of mother. She broke several ribs and a couple of fingers, but she made the horse go over the jump before going to the hospital. The Dahner Boot

Helen Hetherington (Mother) Jumping

Company made an enlarged boot for her right leg. The doctor told her that if she ever broke the right enlarged leg she wouldn't make it to the hospital. That didn't slow her down a bit. She continued to ride and jump until World War II.

Consecration of Beauty

Those whose faces are fair and are in other ways also attractive have a great power over human hearts and lives. A power which it is as necessary to consecrate as money or time. A beautiful face should always lead our thoughts to God, and the owner of the face should so live that this connection shall always be made. How we loved her. My mother was one in a million. She predicted the future. After World War II, I wanted to learn to fly an airplane. I had flown in a plane some 80 times but had never landed in a plane, being a paratrooper in the war. She said, "Clark, you must know how to fly. In the near future airplanes will travel two or three times faster and further. If you don't know how to fly, you will miss so much of the future adventure of your life." Her teaching and advice were intelligently psychic.

My father was the most wonderful man. He lived, loved and died for his family. He was only 5'9" but had a huge heart and was loved by everyone. He had a great sense of humor and the best personality. He became cashier of the

First National Bank and also had built speculation houses for sale. He later became Vice President of the City

National Bank. The university professors loved to come to town and have lunch with him. One day a professor stopped to talk to dad and then ask, "Bill, what direction was I going when we met?" Dad answered, "Professor, to the West." The professor thought and then said, "Good, then I've had lunch." My father was loved by all at Oklahoma University -- including, town people, farmers, ranchers and Indians. It was very difficult and sad to lose such a wonderful man and father at the age of 53.

There could be nothing more precious and rewarding than the deep love with your mother and father. It didn't take words, and I could look in their eyes and we both knew. Dad gave me a poem before I went overseas in World War II. It expressed how a father rehearses what to say when his son leaves to war as his father had done before. When the moment came, he clasped his son's hand and said one word, "Goodbye". My father was telling me with love and good luck.

Dad loved to dream up little poems and quips. "George Washington was a good old sole, he crossed the Delaware with rowboat and pole. He waded in the ice and slush and crushed the British clear to mush." He helped me get started

5

in my business career, and he died before we could start a building company together.

William Leslie Hetherington
(Father) in Suit

My brother, Charles, was 18 months older than I and was a genius. He received two degrees in three years from the University of Oklahoma, had a scholarship to MIT, taught at MIT, and received a Doctorate's degree at MIT in Chemical Engineering. He advised me to get into business school and not engineering. He said, "Bud, you are a dumb bastard." He completed an unfinished Einstein formula in his sleep, got out of bed and wrote it down. It was acknowledged the next day in Professor Courts's university math class.

Charles constructed the Canadian Peace River Valley Pipe Line in temperatures of 60 degrees below 0. He designed all the equipment, clothes, heating stations and completed the project in three years. He became President and CEO of Canadian Pacific Oil Co. He drilled for oil in the Arctic islands and Arctic Sea. A lot of his work was done beyond the North Pole. He found enough oil and gas to last Canada forever, but the problem of getting it out was tremendous. He built a two-shell tanker and with an ice-breaker, went through 30 and 40 feet of ice to get a tanker load of oil. A pipeline would be too expensive. After so many years, it was mandatory that he become a Canadian citizen.

Charles loved polo and was a good one-goal player. His eyesight was very bad. He wore "Coke bottom" glasses, and he was sure he never fouled. He was President of the El Dorado Polo Club for many years and was responsible for building their new clubhouse. Carlton Beal furnished funds to complete the clubhouse. He was also President of the Calgary Polo Club for many years and helped with the club's advancement. A permanent memorial stands to honor Charles at the Calgary club. A handsome painting of Charles hangs in the clubhouse. After retirement he became bored, drank too much, and died before his time.

Charles Hetherington in Suit   Charles Hetherington at Oil Well

I went to four different grade schools prior to junior high school. We grew up in the tough part of town. You'd better know how to fight, or be smart enough not to. Dad bought me a pair of boxing gloves. I challenged every kid within three blocks. The fourth block was a mistake. An Indian beat the heck out of me. Oh well, a learning process.

Tackle football at Andrews Park was a ritual every Saturday morning. One kid would have a helmet, another shoes, but no pads. Usually, we played barefooted. A large Indian got mad at me for tackling him. He gave me a post-game fist to the head. We both played again every Saturday. I liked the body contact in both football and polo. Kids those days grew up rather physical. Children got more exercise and played

8

outdoors. Television and computers of today lead children to obesity, bad health and eyesight.

Mother started me riding at an early age and had me hitting a polo ball in 1929. I spent hours hitting on the wooden horse in a wired cage at the University stables. I would run across town from school, put on my boots, grab my mallet and run another three miles to hit in the practice cage until dark. I did this for years. Through my mother's connections, I was allowed to play on the University of Oklahoma Freshman Polo Team for several years before entering the University. The Army officers left a horse every summer for me to stick and ball. My parents bought me a great 15-hand horse, and we both learned to play polo at the same time. I never dreamed I would be involved with polo for some 50 years.

At that time, the State of Oklahoma would have dust storms that would black out the sun and go several thousand feet high in the sky. Later lakes were built and farmers and ranchers learned how to terrace the land and the dust storms stopped. In junior high school I wrote this poem:

"Oklahoma, the land we love.
All you see is dust above.
You wake at morn to a day so bright.
Within an hour it is dark as night.
What is the cause of our sad plight

That changes to woe our delight.

It's man's own selfish greed for gain.

He plowed the fields to get more grain.

To other lands and other nations,

he has gone to seek his rations."

My mother, Helen Hetherington and a lovely lady and rider by the name of Ina Annette Ewing, taught the ladies equitation classes at the University of Oklahoma as a hobby. Prior to World War II, the universities had ROTC programs, using government horses for horse-drawn artillery or cavalry. Most of the horses came from Fort Reno in western Oklahoma, close to a city called El Reno. The fort usually had 30,000 to 40,000 horses.

One year in the early 1900's, the government sent a horse buyer by the name of Wylie ("Babe") Jones to Argentina to buy 10,000 horses. Mr. Wylie Jones furnished green polo ponies for many polo players both before and after World War II. The government had put thoroughbred studs and mares on the ranches in several states. The cowboys would break and train the horses. A horse became

Wylie (Babe) Jones

old on the ranch at age four to six. The cowboy always wanted to start new horses, as they got $50.00 for each horse sold from their string. Wylie Jones knew where every horse was on every ranch in six or seven states.

Prior to World War II polo was very strong in the East. Great players like Tommy Hitchcock, Stuart Iglehart, Cecil Smith, Rube Williams, Pete Boswick, Devereux Milburn, and many other great players enjoyed polo prior to the war. Lots of top polo was played on Long Island and at the Meadowbrook Club. The Meadowbrook Club in 1928 had players such as, Stuart Iglehart, Watson Weep, Robert Strawbridge, Jr., and Devereux Milburn, and Harry Peters. One of the best US Army teams played at Hurlingham in 1925, including Major A. H. Wilson, Captain C. H. Gerhardt, Captain P. P. Rodes and Major L. A. Beard. A Captain Peter Rodes was one of the best umpires at that time.

West Team Left to Right:
Harold Barry, George Oliver,
Cecil Smith and Ray Harrington

Polo was steadily growing and improving in the western states to soon challenge the American players from the east. Mr. George Miller, Mr. Jim Minnick, and Sonny Noelke were training cowboys and other good riders to play polo and train green horses. Some of these cowboys became top players in the U.S. Such polo players included: Cecil Smith, Harold Barry, Bill Barry, Roy Lawson Barry, Ray Harrington, George Oliver, Rube Williams, Granny Starks and many others. Some of the best polo was played in the east west matches prior to World War II.

Parade of Ponies
East-West Matches

East West Trial Matches 1934

William Post and the Pony, Chestnut Oak

Prior to World War II, the colleges that had horse artillery or calvary had school polo teams. These teams competed in their conferences and against military schools, such as: New Mexico Military Institute and Oklahoma Military Academy in Claremore, Oklahoma. Arizona University had a very strong team each year. New Mexico Military Institute was very good with players like Gordon Von tempsky, Monk Joel, and a boy named, Harris. Later, Jack Dean and Buzz Easterling were great players. The University of Oklahoma was always strong with players like, Jerry Galbreth, Stratford Duke, Harry Hill, Alex Cheek, Clyde Watts, Raymond Mahhall, Bill Aycock, Jim Hester, B. D. McCambell, Cub Haney, K. Garnett and Ed Ramsey.

Dream Team Left to Right: Stewart Eglehart,
Tommy Hitchcock, Cecil Smith and Mike Phipps

A University of Oklahoma player, named Hal Neiman, was killed while playing at New Mexico Military Institute. A large stone memorial stands in Hal's honor by the old university polo field.

Will Rogers helped mount the Oklahoma Military Academy team. He loved to play polo and often said, "The outside of a horse is good for the inside of a man." He helped

several pony trainers make a living. He would buy three or four ponies from a rancher named Jim Minnick, and then send the ponies back and never ask for his check back. Will Rogers said, "I never met a man I didn't like." Our polo team played against Will Rogers team in Claremore, Oklahoma. One year the famous pilot, Wiley Post, came to Norman, flying an old two-wing plane and landed in the Tull family pasture. My father paid him $1.00 to fly my brother, Charles, and I around town and back. How many people had the opportunity to fly with Wiley Post and play polo with Will Rogers? Wiley Post only had one eye. Wiley Post and Will Rogers were on a flying trip to Alaska when they hit bad weather and both were killed in a plane crash. Will Rogers played polo in California and talked many of the celebrities into playing polo. A Will Rogers polo field exists in California. Will Rogers highly respected Cecil Smith and they became good friends.

Will Rogers said, "The western cowboy has taken polo from the drawing room and put it in the bunk house."

Will Rogers told a joke about a man that said, "I came from a stupid family and during the Civil War, my great uncle fought for the west."

Left to Right:
Will Rogert & Cecil Smith

Chapter Two
World War II

Our University of Oklahoma polo team was playing the Texas A & M polo team at College Station, Texas as the Japanese were bombing Pearl Harbor on December 7, 1941. We would ride in between chukkers and listen to a radio. The game was tied at the end of the sixth chukker. By rule, I should have gotten to re-ride a very good mare. I was told, "Oh, no" and they brought out a wide-eyed gelding. When the ball was thrown in, my horse started bucking and ran through the woods. When I got back, the game was over. Guess who won?

Some time in the late 1950's I met a gentleman who could tell you what university you had gone to. He told one gentleman, "You went to Yale. I can tell by your clothing". He told another gentleman, "You went to Harvard. I can tell by your intelligent look and also by your clothing." He told a third gentleman, "You went to Texas A & M.." The third gentleman asked him, "Could you tell by my western clothes"? He replied, "No, I saw your class ring when you were picking your nose".

Earlier, the university polo was lots of fun. Often playing army or ranch teams. A great game was played on a ranch at LaMesa, Texas. A player there named Gus White, Jr. later became an eight-goal player. The goal posts were oil field pipes set permanently in the ground. No one ran over the posts. The university polo teams' players were the forefathers that produced many of the best, future polo players.

When the war started, this was the end of polo at the universities. The old horse gave way to tanks, airplanes, and more modern warfare. However, the last calvary charge on horseback was made by a University of Oklahoma polo player, Ramsey. Ramsey's company made a horse charge on a Japanese company in the Philippines. Ramsey said, "The flying horses scared the Japanese, and they didn't know what to do."

The university polo players learned to play all kinds of horses. Some of the better horses were put in polo, jumping and equestrian classes. The home team would play one string, visitors the other string for the first half and reverse the pony strings the last half. However, there was a sorrel gelding named Baker that I only played. Baker played in a hackamore, could fly but would dive in the air when checked, slightly dangerous. In one game against Missouri, the Missouri player moved to the wrong side after I had committed Baker. After the head-on collision, Baker was sitting up, both front legs in the air and one eye bulged. The soldiers pulled Baker off the field with a truck. I took a sponge and pushed his eye into position and taped it in place. He was very tough, and I played him again in three weeks. The polo was fun and you learned to ride difficult horses.

Without university polo after the war started, I went out for football to stay fit for war duty as a ROTC graduating second lieutenant. Oklahoma University always had great football teams, but I proved to be a better polo player than football player. During a Saturday scrimmage, a blocking back by the name of Jack Steel blocked me so hard, I went ten feet in the air. The coach, Snorter Luster, had bad eyes and walked over and looked down at me and said, "Son, do you have a pilots license?" Come spring with no polo, I played on the junior varsity football team to stay fit. Quarterback on offense and linebacker on defense. My old highschool coach, Frank Crider, was the coach and knew I loved to play.

Clark in Football Helmet

In 1940, I saw the most beautiful girl walking from the university library. My lucky day. My brother's girlfriend told me the girl was Marian Unger and a member of the Delta Delta Delta Sorority. I had been dating several girls in that sorority but had never met Marian. We started dating, but on the first date at a party in Oklahoma City we could not dance together, and she had to be home by an early hour. On our third date, I invited her mother to have lunch with us and go to an OU football game. During lunch, I said, "Mrs. Unger, I am going to marry your daughter". You should have seen both faces as Marian knew nothing of this. In 1942, Marian was elected honorary Colonel in the annual ROTC beauty

contest. She was given a full military uniform with boots, britches and Sam Brown belt. Every Tuesday, I would lead my ROTC company on horseback review and salute my girlfriend, standing with all the army brass.

Marian in Uniform

We fell in love and she wore my fraternity pin, which in those days, was sort of an engagement. I graduated and was ordered to Fort Sill, Oklahoma for more artillery training. Marian and her mother moved to Denver, Colorado, where her grandmother lived. We said, "See you after the war," but I knew that wouldn't work. I called Marian and said, "Be in Norman next weekend and we are going to get married."

Clark and Marian

She and her mother, Dorothy, came to Norman, and we were married in the Episcopal church on July 18, 1942. My bachelor party was spent on the range at Fort Sill and we celebrated with canteen water and Lorna Doone cookies. We had a beautiful church wedding and reception in my parents home. Later, I found out that I had not told my parents ahead of time. They did so much to make the wedding perfect and never mentioned my lack of communication. We drove to Fort Sill at Lawton, Oklahoma and checked into the officer's club. We got kicked out in three days as a general took our room. With no place to live, and the town of Lawton full, a classmate had orders to leave. I told him, don't tell your landlady. You move out, and we will move in. This worked as Marian made the apartment owner a cake.

George Unger (Marian's Father)

Marian was born in Denver, Colorado and had the best birthday 2/22/22. Her father was a very talented musician. He was first violinist in the Denver Symphony Orchestra at the age of 16. Marian's mother was a very pretty lady and could play any song on the piano by ear.

Being able to play a piano by ear reminds me of the story about a polo player that one day went to the bar to have a cold beer. He sat at the end of the bar by the piano player. The pianist had a monkey with a cup to collect tips. The polo player said to the piano player, "Do you know your monkey wet in my beer?" The piano player said, "No, but if you can hum it, I can play it."

Her parents were divorced and earlier Marian, her mother and her sister, Carolyn, lived with Marian's aunt and uncle. Her uncle, Jack Barnes, had made the run into Oklahoma on horseback and staked two land claims. One claim was downtown Broadway in Oklahoma City. Before Oklahoma was a state, Uncle Jack, owned legal gambling houses in Oklahoma City. When this became illegal, he invested in theaters and Oklahoma City property. The run into Oklahoma was made in 1889. They came by horseback, wagons, bicycles and every way possible to claim land. When a gun sounded, the run began. Those who started early, before the gun was fired, were called Sooners and that is where the name came from for the University of Oklahoma Sooners.

When I went overseas, Marian lived with my mother and father. They loved each other very much and Marian enjoyed the family life. She worked at the University of Oklahoma library. Marian was a great scholar and was declared the outstanding home economics student of the year. She traveled with me from post to post and did not take her last final in one class. The professor said if she took the test, she would have an "A" score and get the Phi Beta Capa award. She was a brilliant student. At the age of 82, she still is brilliant with a great memory.

We were soon transferred to Camp Hood, Texas. I was to command a tank destroyer company as a First Lieutenant, and I was also to teach rifle and pistol shooting, knife fighting and Judo. I knew the importance of these men learning how to use these weapons, and I enjoyed teaching. Some were afraid to shoot the rifle, as the old army rifle had a hard kick. To cure this, I would shoot the rifle off my chin. Of course, there were tricks to safely do this. Many of these soldiers had hunted rabbits, ducks, deer and so forth but in a war, it gets a lot more serious hunting the enemy.

Camp Hood, Texas was a training ground for tank destroying. The idea was to learn to destroy General Rommel's tanks with a 105 mm gun, mounted on a half-track. You could see the projectile in the air after firing. We joked that the gun sight was made by the Mason Fruit Jar Company. Rommel's tanks had big guns to shoot a flat trajectory some three miles. Rommel wiped out several U.S. tank destroyer companies in Africa. I was selected to go to Africa to command a company and was promoted to captain. Marian and I caught a train to Fort Mead, Maryland, which was a training and overseas shipping center. On the train, military personnel could only eat after the civilians had been served. I almost had my first fight on the train. By then, the U.S. Army had figured out a better way was needed to stop Rommel. Again, I was assigned to train and process troops leaving to the European theater. While at Fort Meade, we decided to buy a car. I went to a used car dealer in Baltimore. I borrowed the money from an Oklahoma bank and bought an old green Oldsmobile convertible. I got on the turnpike to return to our apartment at Greenbelt. I was doing 75 mph when the engine exploded and the hood cover came up. The guy in back of me saw what had happened and started pushing me down the turnpike at 75 mph with my head out of the car window. When we came to the turnoff, I had motioned and he gave me a push off of the turnpike. I drifted up in front of the apartment and Marian was looking out of the three-story window. She ran down three flights of stairs, knocking on every door, "I have a car". All of these friends came down to see the car. I prayed, but the car wouldn't start. Marian got in the car and the crowd pushed her around the block and back. I had a good friend at the Army Post Garage. He rebuilt the engine, put on new tires and it ran great. Marian and my father drove me to California in the car to go to the South Pacific with the 11th Airborne Division. They sold the car in Oklahoma for what we had paid for it. My many applications for paratroop training were refused. Finally an order came through not to refuse company grade officers applying for airborne training. Two days later, Marian and I were in Fort Benning, Georgia. Family members were not suppose to accompany officers on transfers, but Marian stayed with me until I was shipped to the South Pacific from California. I was in a class of 1,500 paratroopers, learning to jump and get fitness training.

Would you believe? With war going on, polo appears in Southern Pines. A great man by the name of Fred Tejan kept 20 or 30 polo ponies in Claremore, Oklahoma for rent. He had his ponies at Southern Pines, playing polo on Sunday and renting the ponies. It was civilians against army, however, Fred and I, were very close friends so I always played on the civilian team. One Sunday, my old University of Oklahoma polo coach, Captain Wingfield, showed up to play. He hadn't been the most popular person. The polo players called him, Bitchfield behind his back. True to normal, Captain Wingfield declared that I was illegal to play on a civilian team, and he made a big issue of it. Fred didn't have enough civilian players anyway, so I played on the civilian team. I thought what a wonderful opportunity. Paratroopers run ten miles a day with a full pack. Talk about being fit and tough. The captain's wife sat in the car with Marian. Mrs. Wingfield said to Marian, "Your husband is trying to kill my husband." Marian said, "Oh, he is only doing what your husband taught him." All of the players were trying to help Fred make it. One Sunday, Fred saw the feedman coming, and he crawled under a haystack. The feedman asked where is Mr. Tejan? Everybody said they didn't know or when he'd be back. The feedman sat down on the haystack and an hour later he left. We pulled Fred out from under the hay, and he had turned purple. Another week, Fred had broken a couple of ribs, working with a cow. Fred said, "Clark, I can't hit at all but I must play to have four on the one team." He said, "When the ball comes back, I will holler, I've got it, but then you come back and get the ball." To get Fred on the horse, the barn had the usual rope and pulley to raise hay bales to the loft. We pulled Fred up in the air and ran the horse up under him. Imagine what a game we had, but polo kept Fred eating. After the war, one of the players, a flight officer

named Frank Bishop, hired Fred to run his California ranch. Fred Tejan was another Will Rogers with a contagious laugh. Fred shipped his ponies to Linville. A gentleman from Venezuela named Eugene Mendosa, Jr., and a friend contacted Fred about buying some of the ponies. Fred wanted me to come and show the ponies to Mr. Mendosa. I had just received orders to go to Fort Bragg to command a paratroop company. I had a few days, called delay in route. Marian and I went to Linville and helped Fred

Fred Tejan

sell some of the ponies. One week after I returned home from seven months of occupying Japan at the end of the war, I received a wire from Mr. Mendosa offering to hire me as polo coach for the country of Venezuela. A revolution in Venezuela ended this, and we didn't go. Thank the Lord.

But back to the war, I was sent to Fort Bragg to command a paratroop company at the rank of captain. One weekend, I made nine parachute jumps to devise a method of getting out of the parachute before hitting the ground. We needed to jump from the lowest altitude and get out of the chute quickly. Later the chutes had a quick release.

We shipped to the South Pacific from California, and headed to the Phillippines and Okinawa. A little later the bombs were dropped on Japan, and the war ended as we were preparing to jump into and invade Japan. That would have cost at least one million lives. I spent seven months occupying Japan and became a battalion commander, as a major. All bombs and weapons we threw in the ocean. We burned 350 zero fighter planes. When our work slowed down, we got Japanese race horses, had mallets made and played polo on a grass airstrip. You can imagine what the mallets and balls were like. Some of the paratroopers could ride and some couldn't, but it didn't make any difference.

The General wanted me to stay in the army and predicted a war with Korea. When I got home, I was awarded a regular army commission. We readily turned this down and started our new lives in Norman, Oklahoma.

Chapter Three
Post War Polo and Business

My parents had joined the Episcopal church after Marian and I were married in the church. I had taken the Episcopal confirmation in Japan from a Japanese priest. Back in Norman, we all went to the church and thank the Lord, I was one of 500 paratroopers that returned from the war out of my paratroop class of 1,500.

Marian and I had $1,500.00 in war bonds. We got the money by selling guns and swords I brought back from the war. We started an insurance agency after I went to an insurance school in Hartford, Connecticut. While in Hartford one weekend, I went to Long Island polo and met Cecil Smith for the first time. My first three secretaries got pregnant. I was only guilty of one....Marian was my first secretary. I finally hired a real old lady and darn if she didn't marry the mailman. I bought a small insurance agency from a gentleman who had more whiskey bottles in the file than he had insurance policies. One policy was on the local bootleggers house. The company said, "Leave it alone," but I was very afraid of the risk. Nine months later, the policyholder, Mr. Fischer, called and said, "My competition burned my house down." He wanted me to come across the river and insure his mother's house. I called the company and they told me to go out and take the application, and they would turn it down. Mr. Fischer had killed two men; one his brother, and he always carried a gun. I went out, green as a gourd. The first question on the application form, "Is this house a frame or brick house"? I asked, "Is this a frame? Mr. Fischer immediately jumped up and hollered, "I told you, it were no frame, I was burned out." I got out unscathed, and the company turned down the application.

I had played a lot of golf before the war and had become a scratch player. I won the city championship several times and won some money on the golf circuit. I thought I could turn pro. Marian cashed in a war bond and gave me $500.00 to go gamble with the top pros coming to Oklahoma City for a tournament. I was back in two days and lucky to have my car and clubs. We would have starved to death on my golf game.

Our insurance business grew rapidly, but I was impatient and wanted to progress faster and get back into polo. I predicted that home development would be very successful west of the university. Keep in mind we now have $1,000.00 in war bonds. I put $500.00 down on a farm west of the university, and then sold enough lots to pay for the streets, utilities and so forth. We did quite well, but I wanted to also build and sell houses on the lots and not just sell the lots. A friend, Ed Cole, put up $250,000.00 on a handshake. No paperwork. First week, $200,000.00 came wrapped in a magazine sheet with a note, there would be $50,000.00 more next week. Ed was to get a percent of the profits. The project was very successful. I repaid Ed his $250,000.00 and his percent of the profits. Can you imagine, no written agreement of any kind, just a handshake? Ed then offered to give me $1 million on any project I wanted. Fortunately, I had made enough of a profit and did not need any additional financing to continue my development and construction business. I built over 3,000 houses in this area and bought two more farms to develop. We built an office building to house our insurance agency, the development and construction company, and six to ten real estate salesmen.

We later started building and developing in several states. Over the years, we had eight different company airplanes. I would upgrade the airplanes every few years. We started building restaurant buildings for companies in the United States. Norman Brinker and I were very good friends and our company built several restaurant buildings for Norman.

We had a sad situation occur in our construction department. One of our Building Superintendents, named J. D. had married an Indian girl, and they lived in a small house on the Indian reservation, just east of Norman. I had several Indians working in the construction company. The Indians were my friends and I was always welcome on the reservation. A convict had taken refuge in the reservation where he felt safe and hidden. One night, several Indians, the convict and my man, J. D., had a big dice game in J. D.'s house. J. D. won all the money. When the game broke up, the convict came back and killed J. D. and burned the house down, with J. D.'s body still in the house. I was advised of this by one of my Indian friends. I took blankets and food supplies to J. D.'s wife. There I learned the true story.

Now back we go to the wild west. I returned to Norman, went to the Sheriff and told him the story and that I would be wearing my guns and looking for the convict. The Sheriff said, "Okay, but keep me posted." All of my earlier pistol training and accuracy gave me confidence. The convict knew I was looking for him. We had to be very careful and protect our family. We couldn't let the children walk home from school. The Indians were so afraid of the convict that they would not tell me where he was. He came to town one day, stole something and luckily was arrested and again back in jail. The sheriff told me, "Clark, now please take the guns off."

Back to construction and thinking of polo. One day, I asked Marian if I could go to El Reno and buy one green pony and start my polo again. Of course, I came back with three ponies. No stables or tack, but we were started. I had played a lot of polo but knew very little about all the necessities for keeping and training the ponies. Keep in mind, all of my play had been on army horses and they had five soldiers to take care of each horse and mount me. How I loved training the ponies, getting tack and dreaming of fun and my future in polo. I could stick and ball the ponies but had no polo in Oklahoma for training. At first, Marian was grooming and changing my saddles and bridles and in 102 degree temperature. After one game, Marian said to me, "I noticed all the other players have professional help, and their wives are sitting in air conditioned cars." Not much later, Raul Salinas joined our polo family and was great with the horses.

Marian Hetherington Holding Horse

35

In 1952, I learned that a Mr. W. L. Hartman had three or four fields and was playing polo in Wichita, Kansas, which was quite a distance north of Norman, Oklahoma. I called Mr. Hartman and told him I had three ponies and had played some polo before the war. One week, he said, "Come up this weekend, but don't bring your wife or the ponies." I drove to Wichita and spent the weekend with Mr. Hartman at his beautiful Hartmore Polo Club. I stayed with Mr. and Mrs. Hartman in their lovely home. He then told me to come back next weekend and bring my wife but not to bring the ponies. The next weekend, he said, "Bring your wife and the ponies". I had a two horse trailer and would take up one horse and a load of feed, come back and get the other two ponies. Talk about doing it the hard way. It was a long trip. Maybe about two and a half hours each way. Roy "Lawson" Barry and his son, Bud, were there and soon suggested that Roy, Jr. keep my ponies and leave them there. That was Bud's first job and later he became one of the world's best players at nine goals. Eventually the Argentine players thought Roy, Jr. was the best American player. With wife and ponies both at Wichita, it was time for my first game. Mr. Hartman asked me if I could play back. I agreed and on the first play, the ball came out long, past me. As I spurred to go to the ball, my green pony started bucking, but I was lucky and backed the ball on the bottom of a buck. It was fast training for three, green ponies. The next day, Loy Wilshire, a pro for Mr. Hartman, said, "Mr. Hartman, I think that boy will make a polo player. He could hit the ball with the horse bucking". This was the start of a long, great friendship with Mr. W. L. (Willis) Hartman and his wife, Lois. We spent many happy hours together. Willis had a large, Lockheed Loadstar Airplane. We went together to Florida, the Kentucky Derby, Oakbrook, and he took Marian to a specialist at Colorado Springs and solved a dangerous medical problem. He became my polo father. When Cecil Smith was quite ill, Willis took him to a medical specialist who changed Cecil's medication and sped up his recovery. Cecil then returned to polo.

Willis's health had been failing for some time. He called me and wanted me to play in a tournament with his adopted son, Ralph and his trainer, Quadie Guitterez. I took Archie Salinas with me and we got to the finals against a very good team, which included Dale Smicklas, Rich Carroll, and two other strong players. I felt this would be the last tournament with Willis's colors, and it was. My strong love for Willis made the pressure extreme. The night before, I took our team to dinner and gave then instructions of play for tomorrow that probably gave them nightmares. I didn't sleep very much knowing we must win, I had extreme strength and endurance for the game. We won by several goals, had a drink of old grandad with Willis. He was so happy and said, "You know,

Ralph made a goal." Marian and I kissed him goodbye, feeling we would never see Willis again. We were right. Ralph called us a few weeks later and said, "Dad had died." We were brokenhearted with sadness but had so much happiness and love to remember.

Willis' Last Team Left to Right:
Quadie Gutierrez, Clark Hetherington, Marian Hetherington, J. A. Mull, Willis L. Harman, Archie Salinas, & Ralph Hartman

Willis Hartman

Willis never did get along with a Wichita player, named Claude Lambe When Willis passed away, Claude and I were pallbearers for Willis. As we were lowering Willis's casket into the grave, Claude elbowed me and said, "Willis always

thought he had better ponies than I did, but he didn't."
Claude got the last word in, the hard way.

Willis Hartman and Team Left to Right: Willis Hartman,
Ralph Hartman, Loay Wilshire, and Orville Rice.

Willis Hartman spent a lot of time schooling me for a polo career. He stressed the points of building and improving polo. He said, "Don't just take the pleasures of polo. You must work with the U.S.P.A., train new players, have inventive ideas and thoughts to help and assist for polo training." I highly respected his advice and outlined a program. In 1954, I started the Broad Acres Polo Club of Oklahoma. I was the only player to start, however, in two years, we had around 25 players. Several of the old University of Oklahoma players came back and started to play. Each year, we would have five or six schools to train new players. One year, Billy Linfoot, came in at his own expense to help us. I had build two or three fields, but they were not very good. Marian and I bought a farm west of town and built three fields in the old river sand. Many great players thought our number one field was the best they had ever played on. Allan Scherer said, "Only a field in Africa, could compare." We grew our own hay and oats on 160 acres north of the fields. Besides our stables, we built a 48-stall guest stable. Players and teams traveling to other polo clubs -- such as Oakbrook, would stop and stay as long as desired. Our great number one field and hospitality brought many of the top teams and players to our Broad Acres Club. Our new home had two apartments upstairs. Our guests had free stabling, hay, oats and living apartments. Marian was social director and always engineered barbeques, cocktail and hors d'oeuvre parties. We had Raul Salinas to train and take care of the ponies. We always kept 25 to 35 head. We built Raul a house close to the stables. He was very good and one year, went to Argentina with the American team. Raul and his two sons, Rudy and Archie, became excellent players.

I started our sons, Bill and Steve, playing at an early age. Steve was a great athlete and enjoyed other things more than polo but always supported the family polo program. Steve successfully managed our business in Oklahoma City to make our polo program possible. Steve became an outstanding executive and made our business flourish. He continues to do a great job. Bill became a very good player, and won lots of tournaments. He was a strong, accurate hitter and knew teamwork. Bill could have been a good high goal player. The Governor appointed Bill a District Judge over three counties and this slowed down his polo. Both boys have three wonderful children. One of my great polo thrills was winning a national tournament at Oakbrook with my son, Bill.

There were 22 teams entered.

Eight Goal Team Left to Right:
Glen Hart, Rudy Salinas, Bob Moore,
Susie Hetheringington, Clark Hetherington,
Bill Hetherington, & Michael Butler

Clark Hetherington & Bill Hetherington (age 15)

Before one game, I was having a little hemorrhoid problem. What to do? Marian said, "Often people wear a feminine pad and no problem." I said, "Okay, let's try it". I played a great seven chukker game and went home to undress and shower. Something missing....can't find the darn pad anyway. I looked one more place, dumped my boots upside down and hundreds of little cotton pieces fell out. This may work for ping pong, but not for polo.

Someone asked me if I had every been mad at my great wife, Marian. I answered, "Definitely not." An incident happened that was too funny to get mad. I had worn a new supporter to play a game and I was rubbed raw. I asked her to hand me some soothing cream but by mistake she gave me the Ben Gay. I set a new record in the 100 yard dash.

She was trying to say, "I'm sorry", but was laughing too hard.

Back Row/Left to Right: Nancy Hetherington, Steve Hetherington, Bill Hetherington, & Susie Hetherington Front Row/Left to Right: Clark Hetherington & Marian Hetherington

Our wonderful boys have extended our family by adding two wonderful wives. Steve married Nancy, and they have three fantastic children: Leigh, Ryce, and Drew. Nancy is head of an Episcopal parish day school in Edmond, Oklahoma. She is also a superb athlete. Can you imagine riding a bicycle to the top of Aspen Mountain? Bill married Susan, and they have three marvelous children: Shea, Trep, and Kellie. Susan was a spectacular equestrian and tennis player. She won many jumping and equestrian shows.

Two polo players were the best of friends. One player became critically ill, but he promised his friend that he would contact him from heaven and tell him if they played polo in heaven. One day the friend heard his deceased friend's voice coming from above, saying, "I have good news and bad news for you. The good news, the polo in heaven is wonderful, pretty fields and great ponies." The friend on earth said, "What is the bad news?" The voice from above said, "You're scheduled to play Saturday at 10:00 o'clock."

Chapter Four
Polo Experiences

I was very pleased to serve the United States Polo Association several terms as Governor of the then, Northwest Circuit. Willis had said, "All U.S.P.A. Governor's must have projects to aid and improve our sport.

As Governor, my first project was to organize a circuit polo training school, usually held in Norman. We always got a few new players with each class, and Marian's parties were always fantastic.

School Group

My next project was to make a polo training film called, Charlie Chukker, Ray Harrington volunteered to be one of the stars. Our producer, Ned Hockman, suggested we have a mare named Nancy tell the story; which worked out great. Ned Hockman was a talented, famous photographer, producer and director. Ned Hockman is an international honored director, producer and teacher of film and video studies.

In 1984 he received the David Ross Boyd distinguished professorship. Ned was awarded The Joseph A. Sprague Memorial Award from the National Press Photographers Association. Ned's expertise and demand for excellence made our Charlie Chukker and Umpire training films top, professional quality. Ned was learning to play polo at our Broad Acres Club. The mare, Nancy, had to teach a hay seed country boy to play polo or be sent back to the ranch. Through Nancy, Ray Harrington made a great player out of the country boy. Every phase of learning shots and polo were included. Ned spent many hours working on the film to get a professional job. He called me several times at 2:00 am or 3:00 am at night to come to his office at the university. One night at 3 o'clock, I went in my pajamas and robe to assist Ned. Ned was learning polo, but yet did not know the technical answers. This film was great and was used in several countries for training. I took Ned to his first tournament in Tulsa, Oklahoma. A zero goal match for beginners. It was hot and the new players were wet and tired at the half. I took Ned's shirt off, washed him down with water and let him rest. It was time to play the second half, and I had trouble getting Ned's shirt back on and ready to play. Finally ready, Ned trotted out on the field. He was so tired, he forgot his mallet and was almost to center field. I hollered, Nedwin, "your wand." With a little profanity, he trotted back and got his mallet. Ned was learning polo but was a super, expert film maker.

A year later, we made a film on umpiring. Again, it took a lot of time, but thanks to Ned, we had an excellent training film.

I remember one day we were filming an important scene that had to be filmed just right on the first try. To do this, Ned set up three cameras at different locations. We decided to test Ned's sense of humor. After the action, Ned hollered to Camera No. 1, "Did you get it?" The cameraman said, "Ned, I am out of film." Ned hollered at Camera No. 2 and said, "Did you get it?" The second cameraman said, "I had the lens cover on by mistake." The third cameraman hollered to Ned, "Whenever you are ready."

Left to Right: Ray Harrington,
Ned Hockman, Clark Hetherington

Left to Right
Clark Hetherington and
Ned Hockman

Willis Hartman and I started convincing John Oxley to get back into polo. John had played a little in Tulsa before the war. Willis flew John to California and had John hire Kay Collee. Kay moved his family to Tulsa and the search for good ponies began. Kay was an excellent horseman and trainer. He had lost one half of a finger on his left hand but handled horses beautifully and with a loose rein. He was a super back. They bought two beautiful mares: Vagra and Vinegreat from a Wichita player, called Claude Lambe. John's postwar polo career was underway.

As mentioned, the Broad Acres Polo Club was started in 1954. I was anxious to get the Club into circuit and national competition. I had no idea what I was getting into. Two New Mexico Institute players, Buzz Easterling and Jack Dean came and lived with us, and we started preparing. They were both very good players. Buzz was very fast with an accurate eye. Jack was a tough competitor and knew how to play. We started gathering ponies. Willis had sold me 13 heads for $10,000.00. We had to win our intra-circuit and 12 goal to be eligible for the national finals at Santa Barbara. Buzz played one, Jack two and I played three, and we had a shoe repair shop owner from Tulsa, Carl Hall, at back. Of all things, we ended up playing the Witchita team in both circuit finals. We got five goals by handicap for the intra-circuit finals and won by a few goals. Next week, they had

50

a barbeque at Witchita the night before the 12 goal finals. Marian and I took an oil man and his wife, Roy and Ola Smith, from Norman up to see the game and spend the weekend.

At the barbeque the night before the game, Claude Lambe's wife came to our table and said, "The Broad Acres team gets no handicap in the 12 goals finals, and I have $2,500.00 to bet on Witchita. How much does this table want?" Ola Smith said, "Honey, you don't have to go to another table, I'll take all of it." Luckily we won on the flat the same score. Mrs. Lambe said to me, "You told Jack Dean to kill my husband." This was absurd, Jack was young and aggressive, and her husband, Claude, was getting older. These two victories qualified us to go to the national finals at Santa Barbara. I told Willis we were going but had no idea what I was up against. I hired a cattle truck to take the ponies out and back. I had 19 head and Carl's three ponies. I was to pay the bills, and boy did I? The first night we went to dinner and the bill was about $300.00 for the five of us. I was just getting our business going and I was about to get a good education. Of course with our horse quality and our inexperience, we lost the first match in the National Inter-circuit, but we still had the National 12 Goal to play. We played hard but lost again. Because I did not come in on a load of hay, I learned rapidly. When the bills came due,

I would auction off another horse. I went out with 19 and came back with nine.

Broan Acres Team Left to Right:
Jack Dean, Buz Easterling, Mrs. Lois Hartman,
Marian Hetherington, Clark Hetherington and Carl Hall

We loved Santa Barbara, and they gave us a little trophy for showing up. We returned home, had lots of fun and were more determined to improve.

Santa Barbara

After the Santa Barbara experience, I tried to enter every tournament possible. Club polo and sticking and ball are helpful in many ways. You can only shadowbox so much. It takes better competition to learn and improve. We would train eight or nine green ponies every winter at San Antonio. This gave us the chance to play with and against the world's best players on Miller Field and on the Breckenridge Park Field: Harold Barry, Bill Barry, Roy Lawson Barry, Ray Harrington, Cecil Smith, Roy Bud Barry and other great players – to name a few.

Thanks to John Oxley, he and I won several 12 Goal tournaments together. In 1972, John gave me the opportunity to play the winter season at Royal Palm with Joe Casey, Julian

Clark Hetherington and Scoreboard

Hipwood and Gonzalo Tanora.

John was responsible for getting me involved in a lot of high goal polo. We played together several times at Oakbrook. One season, the team consisted of John, Peter Perkins, Bob Skene and myself. Bob Skene had a 90 percent average, making number four penalties.

Left to Right: Clark Hetherington, Bob Skene, Son, Curtis Skene, Friend, Peter Perkins & John Oxley

Harold Barry was a great friend. Thanks to Harold, I played a lot of high goal polo: The 20 goal at Milwaukee and several high goal charity games. Harold, Roy, Sr., Roy, Jr. and myself beat a very good team in Tulsa in a charity game. We dined at the banker's house after the game, the food was great and plentiful. Harold said, "If a man don't fill his carcass here, he never will." Harold declared, "I am taking this team to play the Bermudez team in the Sunbowl at El Paso." The game is suppose to be Bermudez's vs. Barry's. Harold told them, "I am Harold, he's Roy, he's Bud and he pointed at me and said, 'he's Blue'." We played, won and had a great celebration dinner at the Bermudez's restaurant. They had enough food for 200 people. We had a drink or two, and I stepped on the guy's hat when doing the hat dance.

Left to Right: Harold Barry, Clark Hetherington,
Roy Barry, and Marian Hetherington

Harold would bring green horses to Norman and train. One year he brought Wayne Brown and Joe. It rained and we had to shovel the mud out of their motel room. The last night they stayed at our house. In the middle of the night we heard them up and trying to leave, but they couldn't find their way out. "How the hell do you get out of here?" They loaded the horses, got just out of town, had a flat tire, and it started to rain. They should have stayed in bed. Harold and Joe were great friends.

I was invited to play number four on an open team at Oakbrook. We had a practice game in Milwaukee against Harold's team. Unfortunately, I went down, lost my best pony and broke my right thumb. I numbed the thumb with Zilocaine, but I couldn't hit good which cost us to lose the game in the Open.

One year I flew to Oakbrook, not on a team, but predicted I would play in the open. In the first chukker of a game, Bill Hudson was hit in the face, and I played on Dr. Rayworth William's open team against Cecil Smith. Robert Cavanough was doc's number three. He told me, "Don't turn Cecil loose," and I thought , "Oh, yeah, sure." Cavanough was great, but Cecil's team won.

Our Broad Acres team won several National inter-circuit championships. Once at Memphis against Juan Rodrigues's team. The game went nine chukkers, and I had to play a green horse that I had brought along for shipping experience. Don Black met a knock-in, scored and saved the day.

Jack Dean's horse slipped down, but Jack was still riding the horse and hooked a player as he came by to hit the ball. One umpire said, "That was okay," as he was still riding the horse. Umpiring is still one of polos greatest problems. We must be determined for a permanent solution.

Winning Team Left to Right: Ad Black, Don Black,
Clark Hetherington and Jack Dean

I taught Mr. A. D. Black and his son, Don, to play polo. Don became a great four-goal player. I must tell you about taking A. D. to Dallas, Texas to play his first out of town game against Dr. Wayworth Williams's team. Doc played left handed. His usual team was Lou Rames, Granny Starks and Mickey Samuels, about 15 goals. I drove by to pick up A. D.

and he hollered, "Just a minute, I'm going to tell my wife goodbye". He came out some 25 minutes later and I said, "A. D., it took you a long time to kiss her goodbye". Oh well, we were off to Dallas. Before the game, Doc was putting on his spurs and A. D. said, "Doc, there is one thing I don't' know about polo". Doc said, "What is that, Mr. Black?" A. D. knocked the ashes off his cigar and said, "The rules, Doc, the rules." A great start. Doc always brought a paper sack with three balls to each game. Of course we lost. After the game, A. D. turned his ponies out in a corral with the tails still up and the bandages still on. I hollered, "A. D., you still have your tails up and bandages on". A. D. hollered back, "We're going to play tomorrow, aren't we?" It was a trip to learn. A. D. became a good one-goal player.

Team Wives

I became very interested in improving umpiring and became the U.S.P.A. Chief Umpire for several years. I would travel 15 or 20 times a year, teaching umpire clinics. I found at that time that only 40 or 50 percent of the club members registered with the U.S.P.A. The clubs did not know of the many U.S.P.A. services available for the clubs. Most of the major games were umpired by higher goal players or ex-high goal players. They commanded the field by respect but often inconsistent calls and rules are misinterpreted.

In a game, a foul was called on a prominent player. The player said, "That wasn't a foul, I wrote the book." The umpire said, "You should have read it". So much of the fun and friendships in polo are lost by poor umpiring. The U.S.P.A.

Clark in Umpire Shirt

has a great format to train umpires at all clubs. This will take an adequate budget and proper personnel. We must get respect and accuracy back in the game. A few years back a player hit his friend, Sam, with the mallet. The umpire said, "That will cost you $100.00 for hitting Sam." The guilty player rode over to the umpire and gave him $500.00 and said, "I'm going to hit him four more times." The new U.S.P.A. training format will put respect and fun back in the game.

Raul Salinas and I traveled to many ranches in many states, looking for good pony prospects. Earlier, there were a lot of ponies available, and they were reasonably priced. They became very scarce and much higher in price. We bought a good looking gelding that would handle with a boot string on his neck. One problem, he wouldn't play polo.

Raul Salinas was playing on a Broad Acres team in a match and was riding a very small gelding named Yoyo. The pony slipped down and was lying on Raul. I rode over and asked Raul, "Are you okay?". Raul answered, "Oh, sure. Yoyo, he no weigh more than a goat". Raul was a great horseman and a very good player.

One Sunday, Raul and I were flying back from San Antonio after a weekend of polo. I was flying a single engine M model Bonaza. We were above some bad weather and right over Lake Texoma when the engine stopped. Control Center guided me to a very close military field. Raul said, "I know something wrong when the boss he changed color". We finally got home the next day and Raul walked out on the parking strip, waving a sack of jalepenos in the air. I asked

Raul, "What are you doing"? He answered, "I wave goodbye to the airplane for the last time."

Left to Right: Mrs A D Black, Raul Salinas, Don Black,
Ad Black, Bill Hetherington and Mary Oxley

One ranch was 12 miles from the house to the mailbox on the highway. One day a driver from a small city ran into the rancher's pick-up as he was turning around with the mail. The case went to the local judge, who was also the town barber. Before starting, the rancher said to the judge, "Sam, I'd been going to that there mailbox for 32 years and that there city slicker should have knowed it."

With John Oxley back in polo, we played in Tulsa quite a lot. In one game a player was hurt. John sent a player named, Duke Merrill, to get his three ponies and play. I volunteered to go with Duke and help get his ponies ready. He had a funny looking, dun colored horse. I started to ask Duke how much polo that horse played. Duke grabbed my arm and said, "Don't say polo in front of this horse, or we will have a big problem". Then Duke put a bit in a hubcap and filled the hubcap with oats. When the horse started eating the oats, Duke pulled the bit up into his mouth. Duke was a government engineer and very smart, so I shut up and watched. We got to the field, and Duke always kept his halter on under the bridle and tied the halter rope to the tree. John hollered for Duke to hurry and let us play. Duke jumped on the horse and turned on a quick run. One problem, the horse was still tied to the tree. Down went the horse and Duke. Oh well, we had a fun game, and I met a horse that could understand English. Duke was a wonderful guy. One year he sent me a photo of Cecil Smith and Will Rogers and said, "For your support of polo you have now qualified to own this photo."

Teams would come to Norman to play and Marian always organized a barbeque party and sometimes had a western band and dance on the black top road going to the stables. One weekend, Julian Ralston brought a team, including his two sons, Bill and Gene. Bill went down, the pony's neck was broken and they lost a good horse that they had raised and loved. That night, Julian got on the band's microphone,

Clark on Horse

lamenting the loss of the horse. Julian had a few too many scotches. John Oxley was there and he and Julian had never loved each other. John took the mic away from Julian and said, "I'm sorry about your damn horse, but Julian is a lying SOB and so forth." To stop that, I had the band play the National Anthem and everybody stood up and John quit talking. John was John.

Oxley Team Left to Right:
L. C. Smith, Kay Collee, Clark Hetherington,
Mrs. Smith, Mrs. Sherman, John Oxley,
Buddy Linfoot, and George Sherman

We had a doctor that played with us, and he told the story about one of his female patients that was slightly forgetful. One day she walked into an office and took off all of her clothes and then later asked, "Did you find anything?. The answer was, "I don't know, I'm your attorney".

Chapter Five
Notables

I love good horses and good people. My father, William Leslie Hetherington, had always stressed the joys and importance of good friends. I was blessed to have so many friends in the world of polo. In appreciation, I want to make a brief acknowledgment to many of these wonderful people. It's impossible to list them all, and I apologize to friends not mentioned.

After the war, thanks to Willis Hartman, I met Paul Butler. Paul had a great facility at Oakbrook. Thirteen watered polo fields, guest stables, and he sure knew how to organize. He brought polo back big time after the war. When I was playing at Oakbrook, occasionally he would call me and say, "This is Paul, you will be at my house at 7:30 am for breakfast." One day, he called us in Florida from Chicago and said, "I want you and Marian to have lunch with me at the B and T Club in Florida at noon". Paul was always building and looking to the future. His contributions to polo are immeasurable. One winter in Florida, he called me and said, "We must have croquet at the Palm Beach Polo and Country Club." I want you to help me get it started. I wasn't a croquet fan, but if

Paul Butler wanted to start croquet at the club, we went to work. We were very successful. The pitches were built and overnight there were some 50 players. A big party was held to celebrate our success. Paul made a very nice welcoming speech. Paul was always very regal and eloquent. He then said, "Clark was a big help, and I want him to say a few words." I had just broken my right leg playing polo. After my short speech, a lady in the front row asked me, "How did you break your leg?" I answered, "I tripped over one of the wickets." Oh well, it was a croquet party. Paul, thanks for being a friend. His death was a tremendous loss to his family and friends.

Later a nice gentleman, named Gary Lee Weltner, became the Volunteer Croquet Director at Palm Beach Polo and Country Club. Gary increased the number of players tremendously. He added to the fun with a martini tent and several great parties each year. Gary is a quiet and very efficient leader.

John Oxley was one of my best friends. John was born July 26, 1909 on a ranch near Bromite, Oklahoma. He was one of five children. Enduring a childhood of poverty, he made his way to Tulsa in his late teens. He got a job as an assistant to a photographer. That's where he met and later married Mary. In highschool, he got a job in the America

Petroleum Accounting Department in 1939. The salary was $100.00 a week, seven days a week.

John grew up on horseback and loved thoroughbred horses. He and Mary acquired two thoroughbreds, named Chris and Judy, around 1939. They enjoyed riding and John found polo when riding through Mohawk Park in Tulsa. He bought some ponies from the Oklahoma Military Academy and began playing in the park with Duke Merrill, Carl Hall, Mancel Fore and others. He won his first tournament on October 8, 1939 on the "D" Ranch.

He founded his public company, Texas Natural Gasoline Corporation in 1948. He later sold it to Allied Chemical in 1956. In 1956, he hired Kay Collee and bought ten more ponies and became very serious about polo. His polo was very successful over some 55 years, and he was inducted into the Polo Hall of Fame in 1993. He worked for polo safety and had several safety helmets designed. His polo victories were monumental. He and I enjoyed many wins on the polo field. He sponsored many high goal players - including, Billy Mayer, Harold Barry, Peter Perkins, Ray Harrington and Bob Skene. He built a new Royal Palm Polo Club in 1976. At that time, I tried to talk John into selling lots for homes and stables to the players. He didn't want to do this. I felt that if players had their homes and stables there, they would be more permanent. This proved to be true at Palm Beach Polo and Country Club.

John won more different 12 goal national championships than anyone in polo history. He won the Royal Palm Sunshine League several times. He brought Juan Carlos Harriet, ten goals, from Argentina in 1967. He won the U.S. Open in 1963 and 1966 at Santa Barbara, California. He flew 36 ponies to England in 1970 and won the British Gold Cup, defeating Prince Phillip's team. His team was Joe Casey 4, Jack Oxley 5, Roy Barry, Jr. 9 and John 2 goals. This was the only all American team to win the British Gold Cup. John won six U.S.P.A. Gold Cups, playing from 1939 to 1994. He probably won more U.S.P.A. tournaments than any other sponsor in history.

Left to Right: Kay Collee, Clark Hetherington, Elizabeth Skeen, Mary Oxley, John Oxley and Buddy Linfoot

At all trophy presentations, John would pat the ladies backs. He won the Queen's Cup in England, I asked him, "You didn't?" The Queen was giving the trophies. He said, "No, but I thought about it."

When I became Vice President of Polo at Palm Beach Polo and Country Club, we became competitors but still the best of friends. The two clubs coordinated games and it all worked out. In business or polo, John would not accept anything but success. He was demanding and tough, but his soft side was there. We were playing a tournament at Willow Bend in Dallas. Jim McGinley from New Zealand was on our team. He and his wife, Thelma, had just returned from Asia, and Thelma didn't feel well. The doctor told her it's probably just a flu bug and didn't properly diagnose the illness. Jim took her back to the hospital, and she died that afternoon. Mary called us at about 5:00 a.m. the next morning, and we went to John's room. John had been working all night, making arrangements to send Thelma's body home. Everybody loved Thelma. She was a great person. John was exhausted and in heavy grief. He broke into tears and said, "I just can't take anymore." This love and softness was guarded by his tough exterior.

I told John, "We have a final to play this afternoon." John said, "I can't play, and we are a player short." I said, "You have Corky Linfoot in Tulsa, sitting on his butt. Send your plane and get Corky, and we will play". Mary said, "John, Clark is right, you must play." Corky came and we played. We lost by one goal, but we all knew Thelma wanted us to play. It was the best thing in the world for John.

My running Palm Beach Polo and Country Club put us on different teams, but we still loved each other. My great loss, not being close to John before he died.

The good apples fall close to the trunk of the tree. Jack Oxley was a good five-goal player and has a great personality. He played a lot of tournament polo with John. Jack was on the only All American team to win the British Gold Cup. Jack inherited the Royal Palm Polo Club and has done a beautiful job of running it. His teams have won the Sunshine League numerous times. Jack is perpetuating John's legacy. Tommy Oxley is assisting Jack in management of the club and being associated with the sport he loves, polo.

In my judgment, William T. Ylvisaker, has been one of the most important people in our polo history. Bill was Chairman of the U.S.P.A from 1970 - 1975. He founded the Polo Training Foundation and initiated the first polo newsletter, which later became <u>The Polo Magazine</u>. He broadened the polo school program throughout the United States. He founded the World Cup and Palm Beach Polo and Country Club and the town of Wellington, Florida. He managed and leased the Blind Brook Polo Club for a period of three years. He also leased and managed the Oakbrook Polo Club for a period of time. In 1994, he was elected to the Polo Hall of Fame.

Bill also played on teams that won the U.S. Open, the National 20 Goal (four times), the Gold Cup, the National

Inter-circuit, the National 12 Goal, the Arena 12 Goal, as well as the Queens Cup in England. He won the U.S. Coronation Cup twice against England in 1973 and 1974. He played on the winning U.S. team against Australia in Sidney in 1976. He was Captain of the Yale University Polo Team in 1946 and 1947. Bill was Captain of the Lawrenceville school team that won the Interscholastic National Championship. As an amateur, his handicap was seven goals. He gave up the game for a few years but started again, played continually and supported polo in every way possible.

Imagine and praise Bill's vision to buy the land Wellington sits on to build the Palm Beach Polo and Country Club. Bill bought Guerry Stribling's management company, and they started building. They built both inside and outside of the Club's some 1200 acres. My construction company built about 250 units for Bill and Guerry. Later, Bill sold the Wellington land and concentrated on the Palm Beach Polo and Country Club. They built ten polo fields, guest stables, stadium, equestrian area, golf courses, tennis courts, swimming pool and other facilities, including three clubhouses.

Many of the polo players and others built homes and stables at the Club and had tremendous enjoyment for many years. Palm Beach Polo and Country Club became the number one polo and equestrian club in the world. Often when I see Bill, I thank him for his vision and efforts. Bill, thanks again.

Bill Ylvisaker

Orthwein Family Polo History. The Orthwein family have been great friends for years. They have a wonderful family and have been one of the most important and respected families in our world of polo.

Dolph Orthwein got started in Polo after WW II when some of the players in St. Louis, who had played before the war were looking for new players to reinvigorate the club. They offered to trade a polo pony for any horse, no matter how bad that potential prospect might have been. Dolph was always a horse trader, saw a good deal and took them up on it. He immediately became hooked.

Dolph, Jr., Steve and Peter when growing up groomed and exercised Dolph's polo horses. Soon Dolph, Jr. was playing and Steve and Peter were grooming for both their older brother and father. The deal was if they got good enough, they could play instead of groom. With this incentive, both Peter and Steve worked very hard at stick and balling and riding so they could play.

In their teenage years, Oakbrook was the center of summer polo and only five hours from St. Louis. The highlight of their season was to go there and play a couple of tournaments. That is where the Hetheringtons first meet the Orthwein family.

Dolph and the three older boys played many tournaments together. Peter played for Cornell and Steve for Yale, respectively. They played against each other in three intercollegiate championship finals. Yale won 2 of 3. The younger Orthweins, David and Chris, also took up polo when

73

they reached their teenage years and had the opportunity to play with their father and brothers.

Now the next generation of Orthweins is playing. Dolph Jr, two boys, Dolph III and William both play along with William's Wife, Tab. Peter's son, P. J, and his polo playing wife, Sarah, and Steve's two boys, Stevie and Robert, are also quite accomplished poloists.

The Busch's and the von Gontards' grew up playing with the Orthwein's for several generations. The joy of playing with family is a pleasure that all polo playing families enjoy.

Orthwein Team Left to Right:
Dolph, Jr., Steve, Peter and Dolph, Sr.

John Goodman has more than earned his spurs. The new International Palm Beach Polo facility will give thousands the opportunity to enjoy or play polo. John is a great person and is respected by all. John has put a big spark of life back in Florida polo. John, the polo world thanks you.

Norman Brinker loved polo and was one of the greatest supporters. Norman and Mr. Bob Payne built the Willow Bend Polo Club in Dallas. Many of the national and major tournaments were played there. Norman had a great restaurant there, being in the business, and we always had a great meal after polo. Norman was Chairman of the U.S.P.A. for sometime and assigned George Haas the job of perfecting the safety helmet. Norman's first wife was Marlene Connely. She won the Wimbledon at the age of 16 and 17. The press called her, "Little Moe". She did not like this name, and said, "My name is Marlene." She was a beautiful person both inside and outside, and we all loved her. They would bring their ponies to Norman, live with us, and play polo. One week they brought Ann Jones, the English tennis champion and her husband, Pip. We traveled together a lot to different tournaments. Marlene contracted cancer and we lost her in her early 30's.

Norman then married a German girl. In full dress, the polo players had them walk under raised mallets and go to a great reception. At the reception, I saw Bill Hudson talking to the bride's parents. They only spoke German. As the parents were looking right at Bill and speaking German, I had to see this. I got closer to them. Bill was nodding up and down and saying, "Si, si, si". The German girl didn't really like polo or polo players. That was bad. Norman later married Nancy. Norman and Nancy were divorced, and Nancy became the Ambassador to Belgium.

Norman's injury interrupted one of the greatest supporters of polo. He was inducted into the Polo Hall of Fame and still attends every polo game possible. He was the Chairman of the United States Polo Association. Norman was a great U.S.P.A. Chairman and made many contributions to polo. Marian and I always loved Norman and deeply cherish the memories of the great times we shared together.

George Haas had played years of polo and worked diligently with several companies to get the perfect safety helmet. George has played in every major tournament in the United States. He has faithfully done committee and officer work with the United States Polo Association. He has devoted his life to playing and supporting polo. George Haas was also elected to the Polo Hall of Fame, and he is a dear friend.

Bob (Captain) Uihlein made Milwaukee a polo haven. It was close to Oakbrook and often tournament games were rotated. Many of the National tournaments were held in

Left to Right: Bob Uihlein, Jr., Mrs. Uihlein, Stanley Taylor, Bill Mayer, Ray Harrington, and James Kraml, Jr.

Milwaukee. Bobs sons, Robin and Jamie, became very good players. Robin is carrying on the tradition by developing the beautiful Sarasota Polo Club on the west coast of Florida.

I have previously mentioned W. L. Willis Hartman but Willis was so important in getting polo started again in Wichita, Kansas. The Hartmore Club was a training ground for many great players. Willis was my polo father, and I truly loved him. He was a tremendous asset to polo.

Willis Hartman

Carlton Beal loved and supported polo in many ways, not only in Texas, but as a strong leader throughout the country. He was a very important member of the Eldorado Polo Club. Carlton gave the financing to my brother, Charles, to complete the Eldorado Clubhouse. Carlton's wife, Keleen, has continued to support polo in many ways and is loved by the polo world.

Left to Right: Carlton Beal, Jr., Gus White, Jr.,
Mrs. Jean Schless, Carlton Beal, St., Barry Beal.

Fred Mannix, Sr. has been one of the best supporters of polo for many years. He loved playing polo in California and is responsible for the Calgary Polo Club growing and expanding. My sincere thanks to Fred for building the memorial monument, honoring my brother, Charles. Calgary is a great place to play polo and be entertained. One year we shipped our ponies to Calgary and my team was four Hetherington's: Charles, his two sons, Bill and Pratt and myself. We played against a team, including a chap named Barney Willians. Barney only had one eye.

He would jump his ponies over the coral fence instead of opening a gate. During the game, he caught a ponies head and bits in the mouth and lost lots of teeth. The doctor wired his mouth together and stuffed it with cotton. He put a straw through the cotton and got real drunk. He was a great guy. They had a super party after the game with a bag pipe band in kilts. The leader walked with the regal leopard skin on his shoulders. When they marched and played, they were all rather gassed and the 6' 5" leader was walking on the leopard skin. Everyone was thrown in the swimming pool. The next morning there were six petticoats, three wallets, four pair of shoes and other items at the bottom of the pool. I told you they had lots of fun in Canada.

A man was bragging about his new hearing aides. The best and most expensive I have every owned. His friend asked, "What make are they"? He answered, "About 4:30."

Tim Gannon. We are very fortunate that Tim fell in love with polo. His support is world wide. He asked me for advice on an Open team several years ago. He had a great team and won the Open. His son, Chris, loves polo and is making a very good player. Thanks to Tim, we eat good and thanks for your support of polo.

Bob Skene was a ten-goal player and a gentleman. Bob was a survivor of the Bataan Death March. Bob and his beautiful wife, Elizabeth, were admired and loved all over the world. I played with Bob several times.

Two Mexican detectives were investigating the shooting death of Juan Rodriguez. One detective asked, "What kind of gun was used"? The other detective said, "A golf gun". The other detective asked, "Why a golf gun"? The other answered, "It made a hole in Juan."

S. K. (Skee) Johnston was the Chairman and an officer of the U.S.P.A. for years. To this date, Skee puts two teams in the Open with his son, Skeeter, and daughter, Gilliam. Skee was one of the last left-hand players. He has been a good friend and the best contributor to polo.

Chuck Wright has been a wonderful friend for many years. He became involved with polo at an early age. He became one of the best horseman in the sport. He was ten years old when he started leading horses and cleaning tack for Hank Evinger at the Ivory Polo Club in Chicago. Hank was the brother of Dutch Evinger, who was eight goals and a very good umpire. He worked for Hank seven years. He had the opportunity to stick and ball and fit in games when a player was needed. He had met Ray Harrington when traveling to Aiken. Chuck went to work for Ray at the age of 20. Ray had a ranch at Boerne, Texas where he trained ponies to sell. Ray made top ponies with great mouths and brought the ponies each year to the Houston Polo Pony sale. Ray loved to have a great time. One year, he took a mare up on the dance floor. A chair fell, hitting the mare and she bolted in a dead run through the dinner tables. I was talking to two players and didn't see her coming. She ran over me, I balled up under her and we both went running through tables and chairs. When the wreck was over, my right arm was sticking through the bottom of a wooden chair. I had splinters in my head from the tables but no real bad damage. I played polo the next morning. Ray broke his leg in two places. Ray had the best near side in polo.

Now back to Chuck's life. He worked for Ray for five years. They bought a lot of horses from the Joe Short Ranch. They trained one mare, Ever Ready, that always won the best playing pony and is in the Pony Hall of Fame. Willis Hartman asked Ray to hire Chuck and play polo in Wichita, Kansas and Florida. He worked for Willis 6 years. To play higher goal polo, Willis sent Chuck to Will Farrish at Houston, where he spent seven years. In the last game of the season at the Royal Palm Polo Club in 1977, Chuck had a wreck that ended his polo career. He won the Silver Cup three times and played in the Open four times. A great person, horseman and friend.

George Oliver was a super horseman and rated at nine goals. He was the captain of the American Team, playing the Cup of Americas in Argentina. He helped me in so many ways when I was directing polo at the Palm Beach Polo and Country Club. George was an aide to General Swing in the 11th Airborne Division during the war. Another paratrooper. One day he called me and said, "Let's go find Frank, the stable manager." He gave Frank a brand new box of cigars. We drove around the polo fields and then I took him to his car and told him goodbye. He would never think of telling you he was ill. He never complained. I didn't know that would be my last goodbye to George. He went to his ranch in Florida and passed away a few weeks later. He was a great player and had won every major tournament in the United States. He had also played all over the world. I miss my friend. To honor him a bronze plaque is set in the stadium.

One year Cecil Smith was hurt so Paul Butler hired George to play in Cecil's place. At the half of the game, Paul told George, "Cecil always puts the ball on my right side and you are hitting it to my left side." George said, "Paul, that's why he's ten goals and I'm nine goals."

George Oliver

Dr. Rayworth Williams from Dallas, Texas was a good, left-handed player. He supported polo for years and won the Open. We played against each other many times. I played on his Open team when one of his players was hurt. Doc was a great friend and good for polo.

Dr. Rayworth Williams

Doc's Team Left to Right: Billy Mayer, Buddy Combs,
Unknown Female, Ray Harrington and Dr. Williams

One day, I was observing a player trying to teach a beginner to play polo. The instructor turned to me and said, "Clark, what can I do. This guy isn't learning at all." I asked, "Why?" The instructor said, "He's just dumb." "He can't spell cat even if I spot him the C and the T."

The Barry Family were all great friends of mine. I had the opportunity to play with each of the Barry's: Harold, Roy, Sr., Bill, Roy, Jr., and Claude. One year while playing with Harold in a tournament, an opponent told him, "Get off that horse and I'll whip you." Harold very calmly answered, "I had a better offer than that last week. A guy offered to take me off and whip me."

One day I flew to Chicago on business. I went to Harold Reskin's office and borrowed his limousine without the chauffeur. I went to Oakbrook to find Harold.

He would soon be riding a horse up the trail to the stables. I drove the limousine down the riding path, pulled off to the side, put on the chauffeur's hat, put on the colored glassed and smoked a cigar. Pretty soon Harold came down the path.

I pulled out and he turned and he took off at a dead run. Later he told me that he had been in a card game with some mafia members and had floored one for cheating. Harold was quite mad at me for pulling this stunt. Harold was one of my best friends. Harold's son, Joe, attended one of my polo schools at the age of ten. I helped Joe get several playing jobs, and he became a nine goal player. Both Harold and Joe were inducted into the Polo Hall of Fame.

One day a player was having a terrible day on the field and had missed three number two penalties from the 30-yard line. The player said, "I've been playing so badly, if I had a gun, I would shoot myself." One of his teammates said, "The way you're playing, you would miss".

Steve Gose was the best supporter of polo. He built the Ratama Polo Club, Fields, Indoor Arena, clubhouse, stables and provided polo for many players for years. Steve financed the American team to go to Argentina to play the Cup of Americas. Steve loved polo and the polo world loved Steve.

Willie B. Wilson played polo in his mid-80's. He sponsored several pros – including, Fortunato Gomez. Willie B. loved to play tournament polo. The first time I met him playing polo, we got into a fight. We became good friends and played in several tournaments together. He started recording songs, but a horse bucked him off and this hurt his voice.

Later, I dared him to sing at a party in Lexington, Kentucky. He did, and darn, he was pretty good. Willie B. was good for polo.

Will B Wilson and Team Left to Right:
Frank Vaughn, Willie B. Wilson, A Friend,
Clark Hetherington, and Gary Wooten

A friend asked me, "What do you call a man that is good in his field?" I asked, "What do you call him?" He replied, "A farmer."

Dick Bunn was a good player and loved to play tournament polo. He won several National Tournaments – including the 1967 U.S. Open, the 1975 Gold Cup and the Sherman Memorial Indoors. Dick built a homemade airplane. The next morning after a party at our house, he and his wife, Mickey, took the plane on a trip to Georgia. Something went wrong with the plane, and he almost made a dead-stick landing but hit a ditch and had a bad crash. They were lucky, and they recovered from their injuries in time. He was a great barbeque cook and friend.

A polo player's wife told her husband that if he didn't quit playing polo at his age, she was going to get him a seeing-eye horse. She also said, "Darling, you know that it's better to be a has been than a never was".

Memo and Carlos Gracida are great friends. They had wonderful parents. Memo has won the Open 16 times. Carlos was one of the quickest players I have ever seen. They both have won many tournaments throughout the world. I believe Memo is one of the greatest athletes of the last century.

Bob Moore was a very good friend. He took a lot of bumps, learning to play polo. We won a National Eight Goal Tournament together with our son, Bill and Rudy Salinas. His sons, Ted and Mark, became very good players. Bob had just bought several new ponies and built a beautiful new home when he fell victim to cancer. His wife, Lynn, was very instrumental in keeping the Broad Acres Polo Club alive.

A man named Robin made very good rabbit stew, however, the law found out that he was mixing horse meat in the rabbit stew. He was arrested and taken before the judge. The judge said, "Robin, what were your proportions in the stew" Robin said, "Judge, what do you mean proportions?" The judge said, "How much rabbit meat and how much horse meat." Robin replied, "Judge, it was 50/50." The judge asked, "What do you mean 50/50?" "Judge, it was one rabbit and one horse."

Bill Sinclair and his lovely wife, Joanne, were great friends. They loved polo and Bill played in tournaments across the United States. He was Chairman of the United States Polo Association. He did a wonderful job and strengthened polo throughout the United States.

George DuPont and Brenda Lynn do a magnificent job with the Polo Museum and Polo Hall of Fame. They both are very talented people. They work year-round and in the summer, take the traveling museum to five or six different polo communities.

We are very fortunate to have these nice people in these important positions. Everyone in polo owes them a vote of thanks.

Tom and Donna Wigdahl, a wonderful polo family, with their sons, David and John, being excellent players. Tom and the boys played together in many tournaments throughout the United States and Canada. Donna was the Polo Party

Committee at the Palm Beach Polo and Country Club for eight years. She is very talented and a tireless worker. Tom died while playing polo in Canada.

Freddie Fortugno has spent his life playing and supporting polo. He has served the U.S.P.A. for years. He has not only enjoyed playing polo, but has spent hours helping and improving the sport.

Walt Kuhn has more than earned his spurs. Walt and wife, Shirley, furnished the ponies for our polo school at Palm Beach Polo and Country Club. He assisted Major Hugh Downey with each class with no pay. He taught many to ride and play polo, including his three sons. He not only played, but mowed and prepared the fields so others could play in Chicago. Walt finally sold his Fairlane's Farm property to Neil Hirsch. Walt, thanks for your help.

A zebra was brought to a Texas ranch. The zebra, meeting all of the animals on the ranch, asked the bull "What do you do on the ranch?" The bull answered, "Take off those pajamas and I will show you."

Dale Smicklas became a great eight-goal player. He was very large and strong. I always said, "Dale could go bear hunting with a switch." In his early years, he was rather mean on the field. I was his coach and met with him several times each year to discuss what he must do to improve. Everyone must love you, Dale. The players, umpires, sponsors and spectators. Over night, Dale went from real mean to the nicest guy in the world. He had great shot distance and accuracy, and with the new Dale, he went to eight goals quickly.

Peter Rizzo comes from a very important polo family. Peter's accomplishments have not only increased the notability of the Rizzo Family, but he is one of the largest contributors to our world of polo. Peter was a good five-goal player and a super horseman. His management of the Royal Palm Polo Club has brought tremendous success. He has worked with and held important positions with the Polo Museum, the Polo Hall of Fame, and for some time he has been Chairman of the Nominating Committee of the Polo Hall of Fame.

He and his wife Gwen have directed the publishing of the Player's Edition of the Polo Magazine. After David Cummings resigned as Director of the U.S.P.A., Peter has found time to utilize his knowledge and expertise doing the Director's duties for the U.S.P.A. I have worked with Peter and know he is very capable and intelligent. The polo world owes Peter many thanks for his continuous efforts in our behalf.

John Armstrong, with sons, Stuart and Charlie, have played and supported polo for many years. John's other son, Tommy, came to Norman and lived with us and played polo. We loved him. He would come in from riding and Marian would give him a big piece of cake with ice cream on it. Then at dinner, she would fix him a big steak, potatoes, another huge piece of cake and ice cream. He stayed several weeks and then returned to the ranch. When John and Etta came home one evening, they found Tommy had been loading a large tractor on a trailer. It had fallen on Tommy and killed him. It was like losing one of our own sons. We will never understand why

Left to Right: Alan Howard, John Armstrong, Stewart Iglehart, Mrs. Iglehart, Ray Harrington, and Pedro Silvero

such a wonderful young man was taken from us. His family had to be very strong and continue their lives. Polo was a large part of their family life.

Cecil Smith was my idol. He had to be one of the best or the best player in American polo history. He won tournaments all over the world. His wife, Mary, is a beautiful, wonderful lady. His son, Charles, was also a great player. Cecil and Charles were always gentlemen both on and off the polo field.

One year at Oakbrook, I had lost a big game and was lamenting the loss in the locker room. Cecil came to me and said, "Clark, I am ten goals, and I have lost more games than I have won." I always remember his words and he was responsible for me enforcing a new team policy. "Win like you're use to winning, and lose like you have won". Cecil, thanks for being my friend.

For many years a very vivacious man named Jack Cartacella was hired by the Royal Palm Polo Club as Polo Director and often assisted at Oakbrook, keeping time and so forth. I would fly to Florida many winter weekends. I always brought my boots, and Jack got me in several games when players couldn't come. Often Jack would ask me to umpire. He called me Lucky, as I got to play a lot of polo. We were very good friends. Jack became seriously ill, and it was a tremendous loss for our polo world.

Left to Right:
Clark Hetherington
and Jack Cartacella

Six Chukkers of Love

Lester "Red" Armour was introduced to polo by his father Lester Armour, Sr. Red is a perfectionist in everything he does. His riding ability and strength helped him obtain a nine-goal polo rating. He played in all major tournaments all over the world. An Argentine polo friend told me, "I think Red is a better player than some of the ten goal players." Like his father, Red is a gentleman both on and off the polo field. He and his wife, Louise, are wonderful people.

Wes Devon was one of the real nice people in polo. He played for fun and to play with his son, Scott. Earlier, some of the professional players would get out of order during games and have no respect for the umpires. Wes set the rules for pro-conduct, playing for him. One disrespectful word or dangerous play, and the professional was unemployed at that second. Wes would not let a pro-player predominate when they were wrong or out of order. Some patrons would not call the shots and insist on proper conduct from the playing professionals. Wes set the patterns to correct this. Polo needs more patrons like Wes and his son, Scott.

Tommy Wayman had a wonderful mother and father. I always said the good apples fall close to the trunk of the tree. Tommy's father, Billy Wayman, was a horseman deluxe. He was the "webster " of horsemanship. A natural eye for a good horse and he knew every trick to properly train a horse. Tommy's mother, Boots, was a sweet, beautiful lady

94

and loved by all. Billy got Tommy started at a very early age. Tommy, Bart Evans and Joe Barry were in one of my polo schools at the age of 11. I always said it must have been a great school because Tommy became ten goals, Bart 8 and Joe 9. Tommy worked very hard to improve and be the best. His superior horsemanship gave him the quickness and the ability to obtain ten goals. He became one of the best number two's in polo. Tommy is in the Hall of Fame and will always be remembered as one of America's best players. His beautiful wife, Rosemarie, "Rosie", knows more about polo than some of the men.

While writing this book, I often had trouble remembering exactly what year this happened or when I met certain players. The preacher said, "Clark at your age, you should be thinking of the hereafter". I said, "Preacher, I do. I go to the other end of the house and ask myself, What am I here after".

Tommy Lee Jones loves polo and his polo friends. He is right at home and relaxes with the horses and in the world of polo. He was born in San Saba, Texas and knew the hard life of ranchers, and the importance of good horses. I first met Tommy Lee at the Eldorado Polo Club some 20 years ago. He was just learning to play, but had ridden all of his life. We sticked and balled together and discussed the proper way to hit different shots. He wanted to learn yesterday, but that's the man, he is a perfectionist. It was great seeing him play and enjoy polo last season in Florida. His wife, Dawn, is a lovely person. Tommy Lee, polo is great for you and you are great for polo. Keep playing, my friend.

Rob Walton was highly respected on the polo field. He gave 110 percent each time he played. He was a strong eight goal player and was inducted into the Polo Hall of Fame. With his big heart and aggressiveness, I wonder how great he would have been on the very top ponies. He will always be remembered as one of the best American players.

Pete Bostwick was a super horseman and a very fast eight goal polo player. He won six opens and many of the major USPA tournaments. He played for the world championship in Argentina. He won the East Coast Open at the age of 72. He was a Hall of Fame jockey. He rode in three Grand National Steeple Chase races in England. He trained three steeple chase horses that made over $1 million.

Pete promoted polo on the Bostwick field on Long Island. To promote attendance, his motto was "Come watch polo for the price of a cigar". His entry fee was 50 cents. A world famous horseman; he started his two sons, Rick and Charles, playing polo at an early age and both boys are excellent players. Rick Bostwick has brought several new players into the game. The Bostwick family has been very prominent in American polo history.

Pete Bostwick

My journey in life was made a joy by my many friends. I had either played with or against Peter Perkins, Ray Harrington, Billie Mayer, Dell Carroll, Gonzalo Tanora, Jorge Tanora, Juan Carlos Harriott, Cecil Smith, Dale Smicklas, Benny Guitterez, Roberto Cavanough, Chuck Wright, Charles Smith, Rob Walton, and many others.

Polo is a violent game and again, there must be an unwritten rule "When players cross the side boards, all is forgotten and friendships must flourish." To dwell on a friend's mistake is to make a second mistake." I have a great friend that told me one day, "We all make mistakes, but being wrong is not one of mine." What a great sense of humor.

Chapter Six
The History of Palm Beach Polo and Country Club

Bill Ylvisaker is a man of great vision and ambitions. These strong characteristics built Palm Beach Polo and Country Club, which became the number one polo and equestrian club in the world.

Guerry Stribling was the President of Breakwater Housing, which had purchased the Alcoa, Florida company. Guerry is a very strong, determined person. Guerry and his two sons became very good polo players. His father was a professional boxer. The only time he was knocked out was by the boxer, Smelling, for the Heavyweight Championship.

Bill bought Guerry's company and hired him to build Palm Beach Polo and Country Club. Bill was very demanding that the construction of the facilities be rapidly completed. That was quite a task. A stadium, ten polo fields, polo guest stables, equestrian stables and area, tennis courts, swimming pool, fitness center, hand ball court, racquet ball court, golf courses and three club houses and croquet had to be built. With completion, it became an immediate sporting utopia.

I was playing at Oakbrook and after a game, Allan Scherer approached several of the players and presented the plans of Palm Beach Polo and Country Club. He was selling condominiums from plans. Bill's name was on Unit No. 1, and Dick Bunn said, "I'll take Unit No. 3," Bob Moore bought Unit No. 4, Marian and I bought an upstairs polo lodge, overlooking the polo fields. Marian said, "We should be downstairs because you play polo recklessly and will get hurt again". I laughed at this but broke my right leg and had to climb the stairs. I told you she was smart. Some time later, Marian and I flew from Oklahoma to Florida, checked into he Breakers Hotel and tried to find the Palm Beach Polo and Country Club. Allan Scherer told us to go west on Forest Hill. Forest Hill Blvd. was just a small-two lane road with swamps, muck and forest alongside. We found the Club, but construction was just getting underway. At that time, we had to go several miles east to a Quickstop to buy food or gasoline. The City of Wellington was just starting to build. You wouldn't see ten cars on Forest Hill. Don't look now or you may get run over. We were the 26th member to join the Club. Our membership number was H26. Bill was impatient and very eager to have the construction completed but wanted the highest quality. With Guerry Stribling's expertise and energy, the Club's facilities were built. A gentleman by the name of Bink Glison had come into South Florida earlier by boat. He bought several thousand acres of land for Mr. Wellington. Bink told me he purchased some of the land for 50 cents and one dollar per acre. Look at land prices now. The City, of course, was named after Mr. Wellington.

The first polo game was played on the number one field in 1979. A full polo schedule, including The U.S.P.A. Gold Cup was played in 1980. Bill brought many teams and sponsors into the Club. The quality was quickly realized and many started building or buying houses and stables. Marian and I sold our polo lodge and bought a condo on Polo Island. We later sold this condo and built a 4200 square foot home on Golf Brook Dr.

I had already retired from business once and retired again, and sold all assets in Oklahoma except a shopping center and an office building. Over the years, our business had owned eight different airplanes. We sold the last airplane and moved to Palm Beach Polo and Country Club for our permanent residence. Marian had drawn the basic plan of our house, and we built it ourselves and love it.

Peter Brandt and his White Birch Team became a very important part of Palm Beach Polo and Country Club. Peter is a highly competitive person and was responsible for raising both the player and horse quality. With Gonzalo and Alfonso Pieres they brought top ponies from Argentina and set a very high standard. If others wanted to win at Palm Beach Polo and Country Club, they had to match this excellence, and the battle was on. Each year, the patrons brought better players and horses to match White Birch. At first, some of the Argentine players thought they could win in the United States with second grade ponies. They learned the hard way. When Alfonso Pieres first came, he was eight goals, extremely quick and had ten goal potential but would lose his mental cool. We were good friends, and I became his psychiatrist. A little later he told me, "I fire you as my psychiatrist, as Mariano Aguerre needs you more than I do". I didn't help Mariano, but they both became ten goal players.

Palm Beach Polo and Country Club brought back the lost high social life and regality with polo. Celebrities from all over the world came. Ladies, beautifully dressed, large hats and many parties. Every Sunday, several ladies would make their stadium appearance at the end of the first chukker to exhibit their finery and blow kisses to their friends. This regality of polo helped attract sponsors to polo.

Building Palm Beach Polo and Country Club, Bill Ylvisaker had accomplished the impossible. He was ready to use his midas touch and ambitions to build a new business. Palm Beach Polo and Country Club was sold to the Landmark Company.. The Landmark Company was owned by a man named Jerry Barton. I knew Jerry in Oklahoma and our insurance agency wrote some of Jerry's insurance policies. He had either built or bought several golf courses and country clubs. Most of his officers had been golf pros and had managed country clubs. Chris Cole and Steve Braley were bright, young and personable executives. Chuck Fairbanks was a company vice president. Chuck had been the head football coach at the University of Oklahoma. He was smart and highly qualified. Joe Walser was a vice president and we had played against each other in several golf tournaments.

After two years of ownership, Landmark, needed an experienced business person familiar with polo and that knew all of the polo people in the country. One Friday afternoon, Chris Cole and Steve Braley called and asked me to have a drink with them in the golf t.v. room. They asked me if I would come out of retirement and be vice president of polo and equestrian. I had moved here to relax and play polo. After asking what they wished to accomplish, I agreed and went to work five days later as Vice President of Polo and Equestrian. This was the last thing in the world that I wanted to do but I couldn't tell my Landmark friends, "No". Jerry, Chris and Steve are some of the greatest people in the world. I didn't ask them what the salary was. My interest was to help both my friends and polo. Our goal was to have the number one polo and equestrian club in the world, which included the best tournaments, polo players, equestrian shows and participants. Another goal was to keep all charges reasonable, but work to come out in the black. To do this, we needed lots of big corporate sponsors and patrons. The sponsors became a source of helpful income. We also had to have good polo facilities and a great equestrian center. We changed the maintenance program on the polo fields and later rebuilt eight of the ten fields. To get the best horse shows and participants, it was obvious we needed top facilities. As vice president of equestrian, I asked Landmark to build a new, top equestrian center, and they agreed. We hired show experts to design the center. Jane Eblehair was a great help and with completion, she oversaw the equestrian program for some time. We spent several million dollars to build the best equestrian facilities and later, with Gene Miche's help, our dream came true. We then had the best polo and equestrian club in the world. Success doesn't come easy. At one time, we had hosted over 200 polo players during the season. If you were playing polo or sponsoring a team at Palm Beach Polo and Country Club, your thoughts should be heard. I had an Advisory Committee composed of patrons, pros, high, medium and low goal players and our lady players. This Committee decided everything we would do and the Club rules outside of the U.S.P.A. rules. The meetings were recorded and our secretaries would furnish copies to each member. For many years my friend, Norman Brinker, was our Chairman.

Clark Hetherington with Oaktree Cap & Jacket

Every team wanted to play on the stadium field. A careful record was kept on what fields each team had played on. We wanted the best possible games on Sunday, however, patrons played on the Sunday field in rotation. We had one patron that was a great guy, but he had trouble riding the horse. Early in a tournament, his team had played on the number one field. With three great Argentine players, the team got in the finals. This patron wanted on the number field every week and was mad at me for enforcing the patron rotation system.

Several patrons built private fields. Guy Wildenstein built a good tournament field. Memo Gracida was playing for Guy, and the other patrons thought Memo would have an favorable position on the field. They wouldn't play tournament matches there, even after playing practice games there. Memo was such a good player and team organizer that several foreign players always thought Memo had an advantage.

Earlier, Juan Carlos Harriott was the best team organizer in polo. Later, I thought Memo took over this honor. However, in 1972, I thought Gonzalo Tanora was the best individual player in the world. Adolpho Cambiaso came to the Palm Beach Polo and Country Club at the age of 15. He won the U.S.P.A. Rolex Gold Cup that year. Adolpho became ten goals in England at the age of 17. Juan Carlos Harriott was three goals at the age of 17.

Every top player in the world wanted to play on a team at the Palm Beach Polo and Country Club. The competition increased and so did the salaries for the top players. Had we built a monster and was the fun of polo slowly going away? Remembering the fun we used to have with both teams at Marian's barbecue parties, I tried a desperate correction factor. The teams playing in the morning would be my guests for lunch. After the game, the teams did not want to have lunch together and the umpires couldn't get away fast enough. "We must go to Plan B and something must be done to improve umpiring." Peers umpiring peers is not workable. When I was Chief Umpire of the U.S.P.A., after a game, which my good friend, Julian Hipwood, had umpired, he came to me and said, "A certain player should receive a letter for his conduct during the game". I said, "If you had done your job, you wouldn't have been talking to me." Julian said, "No, he is scheduled to umpire my game tomorrow."

I had been working for professional umpiring for years. With the U.S.P.A., we did build a trained cadre, supervised by Benny Guitterez. For all major games, this is the only solution. The U.S.P.A. has a format on the table to train umpires throughout the United States. The plan is very workable but will take adequate financing and proper personnel. All games, 20 goals and up, should be officiated by U.S.P.A. trained officials.

A club must have financial requirements. One day a player from a foreign country came to my office with a suitcase and paid the club thousands of dollars in cash. Another day, a very nice gentleman showed up to play polo. Overnight, he bought a nice condo, was driving a Rolls Royce and wanted to enter a high goal team in a tournament. I asked a friend of his, "Can he afford all of this?" His friend answered me, "He can't make a down payment on a low-cut evening dress for a hummingbird". He was betting on the stock market. Some did gamble too much to enjoy a moment of glory. A player at another club went big time, bought a lot of ponies, had a lot of fun, but the money was being taken from a financial institution he was associated with, which resulted in his suicide.

A more pleasant thought. For some 15 years, the Episcopal priest, Father John Mangrum, gave the Sunday polo game invocation at the Palm Beach Polo and Country Club Stadium. I bought him a nice jacket, embroidered "Polo Priest". His sense of humor helped make each Sunday game a joy. One Sunday, in closing, he said, "Oh Lord, protect these players and ponies and help us get our income taxes in on time." He was loved by all.

Father John Mangrum and Clark

Our Stadium Manager, was a gentleman by the name of Tim O'Connor. He was very good. Tim knew where every valve in the stadium was. He was a workaholic and kept the stadium facilities in excellent shape. He obtained half-time entertainment and make the trophy presentations very eloquent. He was very pleasant to work with and made every day a joy.

Each year Major Hugh Downey would come from Ireland and teach our polo training school. The school had several sessions and went from January to April. We rented the ponies from Walt and Shirley Kuhn. Major Downey was an excellent instructor and over the years, some 22 of his students ended up playing 26-goal polo. He preached that every team should have a coach. He wanted to have another class to teach coaches. Every other sport had coaches. I agree that the Major was right. Joe Barry became one of the best coaches in the United States. Joe brought several teams from mediocre to greatness. Joe is greatly missed by his many friends.

Earlier, a team from India came to play. One player wore a turban to play in lieu of a helmet. He caught a ball on the head, and it took 15 minutes to revive him and borrow a helmet. Local players had loaned horses to the India team. They played aggressively but had little concern for the borrowed ponies.

Some of my fondest memories of celebrities that came to Palm Beach Polo and Country Club include: Prince Charles and Diana, Sylvester (Sly) Stallone, Bill Divian, Doug Shehan, the Dutchess of York, Stephanie Powers, Prince Frederick Von Anhalt, Estee Lauder, Donald Trump, Maharajah of Jaipier, Dick Smothers, Curt Gowdy and many others.

One of my favorite stories is when Zsa Zsa Gabor bought a condominium at the Club. Earlier, my construction company had remodeled it for her. Later Prince Frederick Von Anhalt came and visited with her. I asked the Prince if he wanted to learn polo, and he retorted, "Oh my goodness, no." One day, Zsa Zsa rode her horse out on the polo field where I was umpiring. She said, "Darling, where might I ride?" I said, "Darling, I think anywhere you want." All of the Busch brothers: Andy, Billy, Peter and Adolphus, played at the Palm Beach Polo and Country Club. They are great guys and very good players. They supported polo in many ways. One year, I needed another team in the $100,000.00 World Cup, and Adolphus financed and entered a team.

Sponsors were very important to our program at Palm Beach Polo and Country Club. Many large corporations found polo an excellent advertising media. Cadillac was one of the major sponsors and gave us ten cars to use each season. Helen Boehm of Boehm Porcelain was one of our best sponsors. Helen would provide excellent trophies and always enjoyed giving them at the trophy presentation. One evening at a very elegant party, a guest was slightly intoxicated. The guest grabbed the microphone and made a little speech and said, "And then there's Helen Boehm and her damned ole crockery". Her porcelain company was known world-wide. Helen was angry and had to be refrained by her company president. Helen had met with presidents of nations from all over the world. She even had an audience with the Pope. She sponsored several winning tournament polo teams in the United States and England and loved polo.

Prince Charles came and played polo at Palm Beach Polo and Country Club twice; once bringing his wife, Diana. Prince Charles is a very nice person, and Princess Diana was one of the most beautiful women I have every seen. Prince Charles told me, "I would like to go to a Texas ranch and work horses and cattle for a month." Then he exclaimed, "I will never be allowed to do this." When Prince Charles played here, we had approximately 14,000 spectators. We had to put up temporary bleachers to seat everyone. We even built private lavatory facilities for him. He was a good polo player and was very pleasant to everyone.

Left to Right: Prince Charles, Marian Hetherington
and Clark Hetherington

I invited Sylvester (Sly) Stallone to come and play polo two different times. He loved to play polo and thoroughly enjoyed his visits to Palm Beach Polo and Country Club. When Marian, Sly and I had lunch together, he was quite the down to earth fellow. He and I became very good friends. He is very intelligent and lots of fun. His studio made him give up polo because of the danger of the sport. It would be unbelievably costly if he was unable to complete a movie because of an injury. Approximately 10,000 people came to see Sly play polo.

Sylvester Stallone and Clark Hetherington

Palm Beach Polo and Country Club had several great women players. They were all good riders and had no problem playing with or against the men. Sunny Hale played in the United States National Open, Gilliam Johnston won the Open, Vicky Armour played a lot of high-goal polo and could ride anything, Alina Carta, Sylvia Firestone, Pat Fischer, Julie Boyle and Deborah Couples were all excellent players.

A very nice lady, named Linda Besade, helped run the National Polo Museum at that time. She worked hard to get the National Ladies Open played at Palm Beach Polo and Country Club. Unfortunately, it poured down rain during the entire tournament. It was impossible to find dry adequate fields. Linda did everything to help the ladies. She borrowed horses, tack and arranged entertainment for the players. The weather never did cooperate and put a damper on the tournament. Linda caught some flak, but she couldn't control the weather. I saw how hard she had worked, and she was greatly disappointed. Linda had cancer and died a few months later. She never complained, and we will always love and miss her. I hope a ladies tournament could be dedicated in her honor.

Talking of the ladies at Palm Beach Polo and Country Club, we certainly cannot overlook or devalue the importance of polo wives. Marian loved polo and supported our family polo program 100 percent. She never asked me what I spent buying horses and we usually had 25 - 30 ponies in the stable. Our sons, Bill and Steve, were growing up during the period while I was traveling all over the United States and Canada, teaching umpiring clinics. Marian had a great little pony named Cotton. She would play slow polo with the club's grooms, and they made up a great rule that she could hit the ball twice before taking it away from her. She traveled with me to many tournaments, and in each new city, she always located the hospital. She would never come on the field if I went down. I would always give her a hand signal that I was okay. For over 50 years we were involved in polo. She enjoyed traveling and made a couple of trips to Argentina with me.

Marian was the best hostess at the Broadacres Polo Club and there is no way to count the number of parties and barbeques she arranged. My sincere thanks to my wonderful wife for her support, devotion and love.

I know one player that every time he bought a horse, his wife had to buy a new fur coat. She had more coats in the closet than he had horses in the stables. Another player hit the ground twice in three days and his wife sold the horses the next day. Another good player brought his wife to three tournaments. She was reading Gone With The Wind and didn't see any polo, nor did she know who won any of the three tournaments. Willis Hartman's wife, Lois, always went out early to Colorado when Willis was playing at Colorado Springs. One year, she called Willis at home and said, "Everybody's calling each other a SOB, so it's time for you to come out."

Palm Beach Polo and Country Club was always noted for its great parties. The annual Polo Ball was a sell out event each year. For eight years, Donna Wigdahl was our Ball Committee. She was a tireless, talented worker. Each year she made something new for each table. One year, she made polo ponies for each table. Again, my many thanks to Donna.

Each December, Marian and I had a party in our home. The garage became a kitchen, and we threw a party that our friends ten years later still say was the best party of the year. The number of guests increased each year, and we finally had to bus the guests from the club parking lot to the house. Thinking back, I remember that several guests brought friends and others came uninvited. One guest was giving me hell for not inviting some judge. I wanted to say, "Why should we invite him? You bring him every year", but being a good host, I didn't say that and just smiled.

Costume Party Left to Right:
Marian and Clark Hetherington

Everybody loved the Palm Beach Polo and Country Club. The best polo in the world and the equestrian center was booking the top shows and horses in the world. The golf courses are some of the best in Florida. The number of croquet players had greatly increased. The fitness center and the swimming pool were popular spots. Thanks to the visions and efforts of many people, Palm Beach Polo and Country Club had developed into a sporting utopia.

One year, the government decided Landmark could not use funds from a financial institution with which the owners were associated. At that time, the RTC was, at will, taking over businesses. We had hoped the rumors were wrong. However, the RTC people walked in and announced to the employees that the RTC would be running the Club and later it would be sold at auction. The RTC people sent in knew very little about polo, horse shows or running a country club. They sent a very nice gentleman to oversee polo. I asked him what his qualifications were and why they sent him. He laughed and said, "Clark, one year in the past, I owned a pet donkey." He cooperated with me and we tried to proceed as normal. We played our polo schedule and the time came for the $100,000.00 World Cup. I explained the importance of the World Cup and he gave me $100,000.00 for the tournament prize money. I thought later that was damn dumb of me. That was my tax money. The auction was held and the Club had a new owner. Remember, I had agreed to help and at a very low salary because of my friendship with the Landmark people and my love of polo and the Club. It was time for me to retire for the fourth time. However, I wanted to leave the polo in good management hands. The first replacement chosen resigned in November. No preparation for the season had been made. To save the polo season, I came back and did four months work in one and a half months to prepare for the season. The next potential replacement was sent to the office, but he really wasn't interested and didn't show up much. Again, we had to roll up our sleeves from early to late.

After a training period, the Director of Polo position was turned over to Calixto "Cali" Garcia-Valez. Cali had lots of polo experience but managing a polo club takes lots of knowledge and long hours. My love for polo and the Club will always be strong. I was proud of our accomplishments and had many new friends all over the world. Later, I was informed by an ex-Landmark executive that Jerry Barton proved the government had illegally erred and the government tried to settle with Landmark. Jerry was determined that the government owed him much more than the offered settlement.

Left to Right: Clark Hetherington
and Calixto "Cali", Garcia Valez

The Palm Beach Polo and Country Club has tremendous advantages to proceed successfully for all concerned. The Club has an International reputation. All of the facilities are in great demand from the many members. Property and land values have increased over the past two years. If the existing facilities are maintained and not disturbed, property and land to be developed will increase in value, giving successful results for all involved.

Chapter Seven
Polo History and Future

Polo may be the oldest game in history. We know it was played in Persia some 500 years B.C. The first international game was played with seven on each side, between the Iranians and the Turanians about 600 B.C. The first Polo Club, Calcutta, was formed in the mid-1800's. Earlier the mounts were smaller ponies, originating the name, "polo pony". It's interesting that there were lady teams playing around 600 A.D. History shows that polo was played in the time of Darius some 500 B.C. Also in the time of Alexander the Great, some 300 B.C.

Early in England polo, there were eight players on each side and all of the players were riding the small ponies. Mr. James Gordon Bennett brought the sport to the United States from England in 1876. He brought mallets and balls and introduced them to a New York riding club. The Meadow Brook Club was formed in 1881. The United States Polo Association started in 1890. The state of California had its own polo association until the early 1900's. Four of the early clubs to join the U.S.P.A. were: 1) The Meadow Brook Club in 1890, 2) The Westchester Polo Club in 1890, 3) The Myopia Hunt Club in 1890 and 4) Aiken Polo Club in 1899.

Prior to Word War II polo was very active in the United States. Many of the universities and military schools had polo teams. The Intercollegiate Polo Association existed at that time. Many of the universities belonging included: Cornell, Harvard, Pennsylvania Military College, Princeton University, Stanford University, the U. S. Military Academy, University of Arizona, University of Oklahoma, and Yale University. Of course, New Mexico Military Institute and Oklahoma Military Academy had great teams each year.

Long Island polo was very popular and became one of the most social highlights of the year. Aiken, South Carolina, became the place to play in the winter. Thomas Hitchcock and his wife spent many winters in Aiken, playing polo and fox hunting.

In 1941 when the war started, there were 72 polo clubs registered with the United States Polo Association. The war stopped practically all polo in the United States. The wonderful equestrian and polo activities at the universities and schools came to a halt. Modern warfare was taking the horse out of the picture. Remember a University of Oklahoma polo player named Ramsey made the last horse calvary charge on the Japanese in the Philippines.

I don't know how many good polo players were killed in the war. Thomas Hitchcock was killed testing a fighter plane. Two of my University of Oklahoma teammates were killed in the war, Cub Haney and B. D. McCampbell. What a tragic loss, and there is no consolation but a historical crime to realize more Americans were killed in the Civil War than in World War II.

Some one facetiously said, "Polo isn't a sport, it's a disease." Once it's in your blood, there is no turning back. Polo clubs started dusting off the mallets, cleaning the tack and building polo strings. Mr. Wiley "Babe" Jones in El Reno, Oklahoma, was furnishing green ponies to players all over the United States.

The United States Polo Association became very active and in 1949 published their annual blue book, showing 47 clubs registered. Remember that when the war started, there were 72 clubs registered. As fast as possible, clubs and players became active again in the sport we all loved. John Oxley said, "There are only two ways to get out of polo: Death or bankruptcy." Proof of the great love of the sport, the U.S.P.A. records showed right after the war, 47 clubs registered and in 1957, there were 71 clubs registered. Just one club less than when the war started. The regrowth seeds had been more than replanted and our world of polo was underway big time. Why was the growth of polo so rapid after the war? Remember, someone said, "Polo is a disease". This disease had been festering and the lovers of the sport couldn't wait to get back in the saddle. However, one of the major reasons for the growth was the strength of leadership from the U.S.P.A Chairman. During the war, Mr. Elbridge T. Gerry kept the U.S.P.A alive from 1940 - 1946.

The gentlemen selected to guide our polo world were very strong, capable and dedicated people and they include:

R. E. Strawbridge, Jr.	1946 - 1950
Devereux Milburn, Jr.	1950 - 1960
George C. Sherman, Jr.	1960 - 1966
Northrup R. Knox	1966 - 1970
William T. Ylvisaker	1970 - 1975
Hugo Dalmar, Jr.	1975 -1976
Norman Brinker	1976 - 1980
William Sinclaire	1980 - 1984
S. K. Johnston, Jr.	1984 - 1988
John C. Oxley	1988 - 1991
Stephen A. Orthwein	1991 - 1995
Richard C. Reimenschneider	1995 - 1999
Orin H. Ingram	1999 - 2003
Jack L. Shelton	2003 - Present

These men were all prime movers, and their combined efforts are responsible for the large, successful growth and administration of American polo. In 2004, there were 265 clubs registered with the U.S.P.A. There are 20 men and women's Interscholastic-intercollegiate teams from 18 states.

The U.S.P.A. had organized and will supervise the following tournaments in 2004:

1. Ten Arena Tournaments
2. Seven Ladies Tournaments
3. 164 Outdoor Tournaments
4. TheInterscholastic-Intercollegiate Tournaments

For all of the major tournaments, the U.S.P.A. will assist with umpiring, trophies and the tournament requirements.

I have known the present U.S.P.A. Chairman, Jack Shelton, for some 40 years. He is personable, efficient, knowledgeable and very determined in everything he does. With this kind of leadership, we can look forward to more progress and guarantees the future of our beloved sport in the United States.

The Polo Training Foundation furnishes the opportunity for more people to learn both polo and umpiring. All an interested party has to do is call the U.S.P.A.

Rege Ludwig is a very good teacher of polo and his class dates are available through the U.S.P.A. and the Polo Magazine.

How fortunate we are to have lived and enjoyed our lives in this fantastic country. My wonderful wife, Marian, and I often talked that we have lived during the most interesting years in history. From the horse and buggy days and ice brought to your home by a delivery man in a horse-drawn cart, T-model Fords, the early black and white movies to the present days of jet airplanes, men on the moon, computers and sub-zero refrigerators.

A country where a young boy can grow up in freedom and have many dreams. Walking to school, playing in the park, dreaming of polo . . .Was it yesterday?. . it seems.

To see a beautiful girl proudly walking down the street.
My lucky day! I couldn't wait for us to meet.
Our love became so strong but war would make us part.
Not fearing war or future, marriage gave our life a wonderful start.
War ends and a young soldier is brought back to his love.
Our family to the church and give thanks to the Lord.
To say last goodbyes to the very best Mom and Dad.
We had enjoyed many days and love, but this goodbye is very sad.
Soon two wonderful sons joined our life of love.
Wives, grandchildren and great-grandchildren . . . a gift from above.
What were the dreams while hitting on a wooden horse.

To race up the field at top speed with friend and foe, of course.

Wife and sons made this dream come true over 50 years.

Loved to win, lost some, of course, but shed no tears.

The joy of my horses and friends made the dreams complete.

I know mother watched me play. She taught proper legs and seat.

The joy of bringing others into this game of fun.

Being a gentleman, making friends, whether I lost or won.

Well over 50 years to love family and game.

What an honor to be in the Hall of Fame.

Six chukkers of love in poetic rhyme.

Thank God this game went into overtime.

Hall of Fame Left to Right: Bill Hetherington,
Clark Hetherington, Steve Hetherington
and then sitting, Marian Hetherington

Chapter Eight
Epilogue

I will continue to have a sincere interest in improving and having efficient umpiring throughout the United States as well as volunteer work and expanding retirement life. As a pioneer of professional umpiring, I would like the satisfaction of seeing a permanent umpiring plan throughout the United States.

A view of my career at the age of 83: It is the total recall of events and people. My life's journey was made possible and enjoyable by my wife, Marian and our two wonderful sons, Bill and Steve. At the conclusion of my career, it is a source of satisfaction to be able to write that if I had the opportunity, again my career would not be changed.

"My mother said, "Polo is a passport to the world".

"My father said, "You are blessed if you can travel the journey of life with many true friends."

ABOUT THE AUTHOR

Wm. Clark Hetherington was born in Norman, Oklahoma on July 25, 1921. His father was Vice President of the City National Bank and his mother was a beautiful equestrian and taught the ladies equestrian classes at the University of Oklahoma as a hobby. At a young age, Clark became a good athlete, played football and fell in love with polo at age nine. Clark graduated from the University of Oklahoma. He was the captain of the last Oklahoma University Polo Team prior to World War II. He became a commander of a paratroop battalion with the 11th Airborne Division at the age of 24 and rank of Major. He built a very successful development, construction and real estate company. He started the Broad Acres Polo Club in 1954. He played and taught polo and umpiring for over 50 years. Clark was known as the father of professional umpiring. He was Vice President of Polo and Equestrian at the world famous, Palm Beach Polo and Country Club. He and his wife, Marian, have lived in Florida for 22 years. Their older son, Bill, is a district judge over three counties in Oklahoma. Steve, their younger son, manages the family shopping center in Oklahoma City. Clark worked years teaching polo and umpiring and on February 20, 2004, was inducted into the Polo Hall of Fame.

Printed in the United States
PP983200001B/2